THE WORD ON

FINDING AND USING YOUR

SPIRITUAL GIFTS

JIM BURNS & DOUG FIELDS

Gospel Light

Gospel Light is an evangelical Christian publisher dedicated to serving the local church. We believe God's vision for Gospel Light is to provide church leaders with biblical, user-friendly materials that will help them evangelize, disciple and minister to children, youth and families.

We hope this Gospel Light resource will help you discover biblical truth for your own life and help you minister to youth. God bless you in your work.

For a free catalog of resources from Gospel Light please contact your Christian supplier or call 1-800-4-GOSPEL.

PUBLISHING STAFF

Jean Daly, Editor
Pam Weston, Editorial Assistant
Kyle Duncan, Editorial Director
Bayard Taylor, M. Div., Editor, Theological and Biblical Issues
Joey O'Connor, Contributing Writer
Mario Ricketts, Designer

ISBN 0-8307-1789-7
© 1995 Jim Burns and Doug Fields
All rights reserved.
Printed in U.S.A.

HOW TO MAKE CLEAN COPIES FROM THIS BOOK

YOU MAY MAKE COPIES OF PORTIONS OF THIS BOOK WITH A CLEAN CONSCIENCE IF:

• you (or someone in your organization) are the original purchaser;

• you are using the copies you make for a noncommercial purpose (such as teaching or promoting your ministry) within your church or organization;

• you follow the instructions provided in this book.

HOWEVER, IT IS ILLEGAL FOR YOU TO MAKE COPIES IF:

• you are using the material to promote, advertise or sell a product or service other than for ministry fund-raising;

• you are using the material in or on a product for sale;

• you or your organization are not the original purchaser of this book.

By following these guidelines you help us keep our products affordable.

Thank you,

Gospel Light

PRAISE FOR YOUTHBUILDERS

Jim Burns knows young people. He also knows how to communicate to them. This study should be in the hands of every youth leader interested in discipling young people.

David Adams, Vice President, Lexington Baptist College

I deeply respect and appreciate the groundwork Jim Burns has prepared for true teenage discernment. YouthBuilders is timeless in the sense that the framework has made it possible to plug into any society, at any point in time, and to proceed to discuss, experience and arrive at sincere moral and Christian conclusions that will lead to growth and life changes. Reaching young people may be more difficult today than ever before, but God's grace is alive and well in Jim Burns and this wonderful curriculum.

Fr. Angelo J. Artemas, Youth Ministry Director, Greek Orthodox Archdiocese of North and South America

I heartily recommend Jim Burns's *YouthBuilders Group Bible Studies* because they are leader-friendly tools that are ready to use in youth groups and Sunday School classes. Jim addresses the tough questions that students are genuinely facing every day and, through his engaging style, challenges young people to make their own decisions to move from their current opinions to God's convictions taught in the Bible. Every youth group will benefit from this excellent curriculum.

Paul Borthwick, Minister of Missions, Grace Chapel

Jim Burns recognizes the fact that small groups are where life change happens. In this study he has captured the essence of that value. Further, Jim has given much thought to shaping this very effective material into a usable tool that serves the parent, leader and student.

Bo Boshers, Executive Director, Student Impact,
Willow Creek Community Church

It is about time that someone who knows kids, understands kids and works with kids writes youth curriculum that youth workers, both volunteer and professional, can use. Jim Burns's *YouthBuilders Group Bible Studies* is the curriculum that youth ministry has been waiting a long time for.
Ridge Burns, President,
The Center for Student Missions

There are very few people in the world who know how to communicate life-changing truth effectively to teens. Jim Burns is one of the best. *YouthBuilders Group Bible Studies* puts handles on those skills and makes them available to everyone. These studies are biblically sound, hands-on practical and just plain fun. This one gets a five-star endorsement—which isn't bad since there are only four stars to start with.
Ken Davis, President,
Dynamic Communications

Jim Burns has a way of being creative without being "hokey." *YouthBuilders Group Bible Studies* takes the age-old model of curriculum and gives it a new look with tools such as the Bible *Tuck-In*™ and Parent Page. Give this new resource a try and you'll see that Jim shoots straightforward on tough issues. The *YouthBuilders* series is great for leading small-group discussions as well as teaching a large class of junior high or high school students. The Parent Page will help you get support from your parents in that they will understand the topics you are dealing with in your group. Put Jim's years of experience to work for you by equipping yourself with this quality material.
Curt Gibson, Pastor to Junior High,
First Church of the Nazarene of Pasadena

Once again, Jim Burns has managed to handle very timely issues with just the right touch. His *YouthBuilders Group Bible Studies* succeeds in teaching solid biblical values without being stuffy or preachy. The format is user-friendly, designed to stimulate high involvement and deep discussion. Especially impressive is the Parent Page, a long overdue tool to help parents become part of the Christian education loop. I look forward to using it with my kids!
David M. Hughes, Pastor,
First Baptist Church, Winston-Salem

What do you get when you combine a deep love for teens, over 20 years' experience in youth ministry and an excellent writer? You get Jim Burns's *YouthBuilders* series! This stuff has absolutely hit the nail on the head. Quality Sunday School and small-group material is tough to come by these days, but Jim has put every ounce of creativity he has into these books.
Greg Johnson, author of *Getting Ready for the Guy/Girl Thing* and *Keeping Your Cool While Sharing Your Faith*

Jim Burns has a gift, the gift of combining the relational and theological dynamics of our faith in a graceful, relevant and easy-to-chew-and-swallow way. *YouthBuilders Group Bible Studies* is a hit, not only for teens but for teachers.
Gregg Johnson, National Youth Director,
International Church of the Foursquare Gospel

The practicing youth worker always needs more ammunition. Here is a whole book full of practical, usable resources for those facing kids face-to-face. *YouthBuilders Group Bible Studies* will get that blank stare off the faces of kids in your youth meeting!
Jay Kesler, President, Taylor University

I couldn't be more excited about the *YouthBuilders Group Bible Studies*. It couldn't have arrived at a more needed time. Spiritually we approach the future engaged in war with young people taking direct hits from the devil. This series will practically help teens who feel partially equipped to "put on the whole armor of God."
Mike MacIntosh, Pastor,
Horizon Christian Fellowship

In *YouthBuilders Group Bible Studies*, Jim Burns pulls together the key ingredients for an effective curriculum series. Jim captures the combination of teen involvement and a solid biblical perspective, with topics that are relevant and straightforward. This series will be a valuable tool in the local church.
Dennis "Tiger" McLuen, Executive Director,
Youth Leadership

My ministry takes me to the lost kids in our nation's cities where youth games and activities are often irrelevant and plain Bible knowledge for the sake of learning is unattractive. Young people need the information necessary to make wise decisions related to everyday problems. *YouthBuilders* will help many young people integrate their faith into everyday life, which after all is our goal as youth workers.
Miles McPherson, President, Project Intercept

Jim Burns's passion for teens, youth workers and parents of teens is evident in the *YouthBuilders Group Bible Studies*. He has a gift of presenting biblical truths on a level teens will fully understand, and youth workers and parents can easily communicate.
Al Menconi, President, Al Menconi Ministries

Youth ministry curriculum is often directed to only one spoke of the wheel of youth ministry—the adolescent. Not so with this material! Jim has enlarged the education circle, including information for the adolescent, the parent and the youth worker. *YouthBuilders Group Bible Studies* is youth and family ministry-oriented material at its best.
Helen Musick, Instructor of Youth Ministry,
Asbury Seminary

Finally, a Bible study that has it all! It's action-packed, practical and biblical; but that's only the beginning. *YouthBuilders* involves students in the Scriptures. It's relational, interactive and leads kids toward lifestyle changes. The unique aspect is a page for parents, something that's usually missing from adolescent curriculum. Jim Burns has outdone himself. This isn't a home run—it's a grand slam!
Dr. David Olshine, Director of Youth Ministries,
Columbia International University

Here is a thoughtful and relevant curriculum designed to meet the needs of youth workers, parents and students. It's creative, interactive and biblical—and with Jim Burns's name on it, you know you're getting a quality resource.
Laurie Polich, Youth Director,
First Presbyterian Church of Berkeley

In 10 years of youth ministry I've never used a curriculum because I've never found anything that actively involves students in the learning process, speaks to young people where they are and challenges them with biblical truth—I'll use this! *YouthBuilders Group Bible Studies* is a complete curriculum that is helpful to parents, youth leaders and, most importantly, today's youth.
Glenn Schroeder, Youth and Young Adult Ministries,
Vineyard Christian Fellowship, Anaheim

This new material by Jim Burns represents a vitality in curriculum and, I believe, a more mature and faithful direction. *YouthBuilders Group Bible Studies* challenges youth by teaching them how to make decisions rather than telling them what decisions to make. Each session offers teaching concepts, presents options and asks for a decision. I believe it's healthy, the way Christ taught and represents the abilities, personhood and faithfulness of youth. I give it an A+!
J. David Stone, President, Stone & Associates

Jim Burns has done it again! This is a practical, timely and reality-based resource for equipping teens to live life in the fast-paced, pressure-packed adolescent world of the '90s. A very refreshing creative oasis in the curriculum desert!
Rich Van Pelt, President, Alongside Ministries

YouthBuilders Group Bible Studies is a tremendous new set of resources for reaching students. Jim has his finger on the pulse of youth today. He understands their mind-sets, and has prepared these studies in a way that will capture their attention and lead to greater maturity in Christ. I heartily recommend these studies.
Rick Warren, Senior Pastor,
Saddleback Valley Community Church

CONTENTS

THANKS AND THANKS AGAIN!

This project is definitely a team effort. First of all, thank you to Cathy, Christy, Rebecca and Heidi Burns, the women of my life.

Thank you to Jill Corey, my incredible assistant and long-time friend.

Thank you to Doug Webster for your outstanding job as executive director of the National Institute of Youth Ministry (NIYM).

Thank you to the NIYM staff in San Clemente: Gary Lenhart, Russ Cline, Laurie Pilz, Luchi Bierbower, Dean Bruns and Larry Acosta.

Thank you to our 100-plus associate trainers who have been my coworkers, friends and sacrificial guinea pigs.

Thank you to Kyle Duncan, Bill Greig III and Jean Daly for convincing me that Gospel Light is a great publisher that deeply believes in the mission to reach young people. I believe!

Thank you to the Youth Specialties world. Tic, Mike and Wayne, so many years ago, you brought on a wet-behind-the-ears youth worker with hair and taught me most everything I know about youth work today.

Thank you to the hundreds of donors, supporters and friends of NIYM. You are helping create an international grass-roots movement that is helping young people make positive decisions that will affect them for the rest of their lives.

"Where there is no counsel, the people fall; But in the multitude of counselors there is safety"
(Proverbs 11:14, *NKJV*).
Jim Burns
San Clemente, CA

DEDICATION

To South Coast Community Church and First Presbyterian Church, Orange: We were blessed to be together at two of the greatest churches in the world. We will forever treasure our relationships and the wonderful memories of your outstanding youth ministries. Your input and influence on our lives has been eternally transforming. Thank you and thank God for the Body of Christ in Orange, and Irvine, California.

Jim Burns and Doug Fields

YOUTHBUILDERS GROUP BIBLE STUDIES

It's Relational—Students learn best when they talk—not when you talk. There is always a get acquainted section in the Warm Up. All the experiences are based on building community in your group.

It's Biblical—With no apologies, this series in unashamedly Christian. Every session has a practical, relevant Bible study.

It's Experiential—Studies show that young people retain up to 85 percent of the material when they are *involved* in action-oriented, experiential learning. The sessions use role-plays, discussion starters, case studies, graphs and other experiential, educational methods. *We believe it's a sin to bore a young person with the gospel.*

It's Interactive—This study is geared to get students feeling comfortable with sharing ideas and interacting with peers and leaders.

It's Easy to Follow—The sessions have been prepared by Jim Burns to allow the leader to pick up the material and use it. There is little preparation time on your part. Jim did the work for you.

It's Adaptable—You can pick and choose from several topics or go straight through the material as a whole study.

It's Age Appropriate—In the "Team Effort" section, one group experience relates best to junior high students while the other works better with high school students. Look at both to determine which option is best for your group.

It's Parent Oriented—The Parent Page helps you to do youth ministry at its finest. Christian education should take place in the home as well as in the church. The Parent Page is your chance to come alongside the parents and help them have a good discussion with their kids.

It's Proven—This material was not written by someone in an ivory tower. It was written for young people and has already been used with them. They love it.

HOW TO USE THIS STUDY

The 12 sessions are divided into three stand-alone units. Each unit has four sessions. You may choose to teach all 12 sessions consecutively. Or you may use only one unit. Or you may present individual sessions. You know your group best so you choose.

Each of the 12 sessions is divided into five sections.

Check It Out—This section is designed for the students to think about what spiritual gifts they may have.

Team Effort—Following the model of Jesus, the Master Teacher, these activities engage young people in the session. Stories, group situations, surveys and more bring the session to the students. There is an option for junior high/middle school students and one for high school students.

In the Word—Most young people are biblically illiterate. These Bible studies present the Word of God and encourage students to see the relevance of the Scriptures to their lives.

Things to Think About—Young people need the opportunity to really think through the issues at hand. These discussion starters get students talking about the subject and interacting on important issues.

Parent Page—A youth worker can only do so much. Reproduce this page and get it into the hands of parents. This tool allows quality parent/teen communication that really brings the session home.

THE BIBLE *TUCK-IN*™

It's a tear-out sheet you fold and place in your Bible, containing the essentials you'll need for teaching your group.

HERE'S HOW TO USE IT:

To prepare for the session, first study the session. Tear out the Bible *Tuck-In*™ and personalize it by making notes. Fold the Bible *Tuck-In*™ in half on the dotted line. Slip it into your Bible for easy reference throughout the session. The Key Verse, Biblical Basis and Big Idea at the beginning of the Bible *Tuck-In*™ will help you keep the session on track. With the Bible *Tuck-In*™ your students will see that your teaching comes from the Bible and won't be distracted by a leader's guide.

Unit I

SPIRITUAL GIFTS THAT DEMONSTRATE GOD'S LOVE AND PRESENCE

LEADER'S PEP TALK

In some ways you might say Doug and I (Jim) have grown up together. Actually, I'm nine years older but we've "hung out" since 1977. I had hair in 1977 and Doug was a junior higher in my youth group who was still wondering if girls had "cooties" and his strongest love was baseball. My first remembrance of Doug Fields was that he was a very confident kid in our youth group who had the possibility of being a little obnoxious. I told him as an eighth grader, "you will either end up in prison or be one of the most incredible youth workers in the twentieth century." Well, he hasn't made it to prison yet, and he is truly one of a handful of youth specialists leading the way into the twenty-first century.

God has truly gifted Doug with several outstanding abilities and talents. It has been one of the joys of my life to watch him be used by God to reach thousands of students and come alongside thousands of youth workers to make this world a better place. However, what has been perhaps the most exciting part of seeing God's hand in his life is the fact that he has searched out his spiritual gifts and is using them for the glory of God.

Doug came to me over 10 years ago when we were working together at South Coast Community Church and suggested that we do a series on spiritual gifts for our high school group. He had been learning a great deal about his own spiritual gifts and thought it was time to have us share what we both had been learning with our kids.

He tested the Bible studies at Community Presbyterian Church in Danville, California and we did a series at South Coast. Today, we would both say that helping students find their spiritual gifts is one of the highlights of our ministries. One such student was Kim Halloway who came up to me after the session on "The Gift of Hospitality," and was so excited to discover that she definitely had been given the gift of hospitality. She realized she had been using it

without knowing it was a spiritual gift, and said she would now actively use the gift of hospitality to serve God. She is still doing it 10 years later.

Helping students find their spiritual gifts and then helping them use their gifts for the glory of God is what these sessions are all about. The first session is about discovery. In it you have the opportunity to invite most of your students, for the first time, to discover the wonderful world of spiritual gifts. Your students will never be the same as you enlist them in God's army of grace-gifted people who demonstrate God's love and His presence through their lives.

This project has been one of those never-ending tasks because over the years, we have continued to speak, write and introduce people to *The Word on Finding and Using Your Spiritual Gifts*. Our prayer for this first section is that you will be able to develop relationships with your students like we did with each other two decades ago. Just as we've grown in our friendship, spiritual lives and our ministries, we believe you can have the same blessing from God with your students.

SPIRITUAL GIFTS: ARE THEY FOR EVERYONE?

KEY VERSE

"Now about spiritual gifts, brothers, I do not want you to be ignorant."
1 Corinthians 12:1

BIBLICAL BASIS

Romans 12:6-8;
1 Corinthians 12: 1, 4-26, 28-30;
Ephesians 3:20,21; 4:7,8,11,12;
1 Peter 4:9-11

THE BIG IDEA

All of us are gifted! God has given each one of us specific spiritual gifts that help in the effectiveness of the body of Christ.

AIMS OF THIS SESSION

During this session you will guide students to:
• Examine the biblical concept that God gives all Christians spiritual gifts;
• Discover which spiritual gifts may be given to them from God;
• Implement specific ways to serve God with their spiritual giftedness.

CHECK IT OUT

SKILLS INVENTORY—
Students list skills they have and those they wish they had.

TEAM EFFORT— JUNIOR HIGH/ MIDDLE SCHOOL
WHO AM I?—
Students give positive comments to each other.

TEAM EFFORT— HIGH SCHOOL
I AM...—
Students share information about themselves.

IN THE WORD
WHAT ARE THE SPIRITUAL GIFTS?—
A Bible study on what spiritual gifts there are.

THINGS TO THINK ABOUT(OPTIONAL)

Questions to get students thinking and talking about the impact of the spiritual gifts on the Church and individual Christians.

PARENT PAGE

A tool to get the session into the home and allow parents and young people to discuss what the spiritual gifts are and which ones they think they have.

LEADER'S DEVOTIONAL

"Now to him who is able to do immeasurably more than all we ask or imagine, according to his power that is at work within us, to him be glory in the church and in Christ Jesus throughout all generations, for ever and ever! Amen" (Ephesians 3:20,21).

As you begin this exciting new Bible study on spiritual gifts, you may be asking the same question a lot of other youth workers occasionally consider: "Am I really using my spiritual gifts to their fullest potential?" Or you may be wondering about the same thing as the young people in your youth group: "What are spiritual gifts, and has God given me any?"

My hope and prayer for you as you flip open the pages to these twelve lessons is that you walk away…

• Encouraged: It's so easy for youth workers to get discouraged by the lack of progress they see in their own lives and the lives of teenagers. God has gifted you and He wants you to be encouraged in your ministry through the spiritual gifts He has given you. Be encouraged—God is with you today!

• Empowered: The Holy Spirit wants to use you in great ways for His kingdom. That's why you are empowered by the Holy Spirit to use your spiritual gifts to build up the body of Christ. You are empowered by God!

• Equipped: Once you discover your spiritual gifts, it's critical to be equipped to use them in the lives of students and their families. God would never give you a spiritual gift without equipping you first. Why not take some time to pray about what the Lord will do through this exciting process? (Written by Joey O'Connor.)

"But our all-wise God has apportioned His gifts as He wills, and one day He will require from each of us an accounting of our use of those gifts...if you and I really want to be used by our Lord, it will pay us to ferret out what our particular ability is, then get busy putting it to use."
—Jeanette Lockerbie

SPIRITUAL GIFTS: ARE THEY FOR EVERYONE?

EY VERSE

"Now about spiritual gifts, brothers, I do not want you to be ignorant." 1 Corinthians 12:1

BIBLICAL BASIS

Romans 12:6-8; 1 Corinthians 12:1, 4-26, 28-30; Ephesians 3:20,21; 4:7,8,11,12; 1 Peter 4:9-11

THE BIG IDEA

All of us are gifted! God has given each one of us specific spiritual gifts that help in the effectiveness of the body of Christ.

CHECK IT OUT (5-10 MINUTES)

SKILLS INVENTORY

• Give each student a copy of "Skills Inventory" on page 19 and a pen or pencil.

• Have students complete the page.

1. **My top three skills**

   a. _____

   b. _____

   c. _____

2. **Skills I wish I had**

   a. _____

   b. _____

   c. _____

(Suggestions: music, computers, athletics, art, photography, counseling, drama, writing, cooking, memory, fixing, designing, etc.)

───── Fold ─────

17

SO WHAT?

If I could design a specific way to serve God around my giftedness it might be...

_____

THINGS TO THINK ABOUT (OPTIONAL)

• Use the questions on page 23 after or as a part of "In the Word."

1. What would happen to the Body of Christ if everyone had the same gifts?

2. How can having knowledge about spiritual gifts positively affect a Christian?

3. Why do you think there are so many different types of spiritual gifts within the Body of Christ?

PARENT PAGE

• Distribute page to parents.

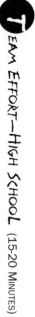

TEAM EFFORT—JUNIOR HIGH/MIDDLE SCHOOL (15-20 MINUTES)

WHO AM I?

- Divide students into groups of three or four.
- Give each student a copy of "Who Am I?" on page 19 and a pen or pencil.
- Have students complete the paper and then share their answers with their group members.

I was born in _____ in _____.
city

The most influential person in my life is _____ because _____.

God has gifted me with the ability to _____.

If I knew I couldn't fail, I would _____.

TEAM EFFORT—HIGH SCHOOL (15-20 MINUTES)

I AM...

- Divide students into groups of five or six.
- Give each student a piece of paper and a pen or pencil.
- Have each student write his or her name and the words "I Am..." at the top of his or her paper.
- Have students pass their papers around the small group. Each student is to write a positive comment about every other student in the group.
- When everyone has finished, ask the students to take their sheets back and share two sentences they found to be surprising or confirming

IN THE WORD (25-30 MINUTES)

WHAT ARE THE SPIRITUAL GIFTS?

- Divide students into four groups.
- Give each student a copy of "What Are the Spiritual Gifts?" on page 21 and 23 a pen or pencil.
- Assign each group one of the Scripture passages.
- When students have completed their lists, have them share the gifts they found in their particular passage with the entire group.

There are four passages in the New Testament which teach about spiritual gifts. Read the passage of Scripture assigned to your group and write the various gifts under that section. Keep in mind Paul's desire for Christians concerning spiritual gifts. "Now concerning spiritual gifts, brethren, I do not want you to be uninformed." (1 Corinthians 12:1 RSV).

Romans 12:6-8	1 Corinthians 12:4-11	Ephesians 4:7,8,11,12	1 Peter 4:9-11
1.	1.	1.	1.
2.	2.	2.	2.
3.	3.	3.	3.
	1 Corinthians 12:28-30		
	1.		
	2.		
	3.		

---

4. _____
5. _____
6. _____
7. _____
8. _____
9. _____
10. _____
11. _____
12. _____

4. _____
5. _____

In God's creative workmanship He designs each person to be remarkably different from all others. As we submit our lives to the Holy Spirit, He also gives a variety of spiritual gifts to each individual. No one person except Jesus Christ has all of the gifts, and at the same time there are *no* ungifted Christians.

Read and summarize 1 Peter 4:10. Explain how your gifts are to be used.

Read 1 Corinthians 12:4-12. Why are there many kinds of spiritual gifts?

How do spiritual gifts benefit others and accomplish God's work?

Read 1 Corinthians 12:12-26 and paraphrase Paul's thought.

Here's a helpful guideline to follow when learning about and using your spiritual gifts.

1. **Experiment:** Sometimes the only way to know if God has gifted you in a certain area is to try out the gift. You will never know if you have the gift of teaching unless you try to teach!

2. **Examine your feelings:** Your feelings are very important! If you experiment with the gift of teaching and feel extremely uncomfortable and embarrassed, then perhaps you don't have the gift (at this time). On the other hand, if you were to experiment with the gift of hospitality and found that you enjoy entertaining people, sheltering them and feeding needy neighbors and, furthermore, if you receive personal joy, satisfaction and feel used by God in doing these things, then you most likely have the gift of hospitality.

3. **Evaluate your effectiveness:** Every once in a while stop and think about your effectiveness. Ask yourself these three questions: "Am I effective?" "Am I having a *worthwhile* impact on these people?" "Is God using me in this particular area?" Remember: God has given everyone a gift that will be effective.

4. **Expect confirmation from the Body of Christ:** Other Christians should be encouraging or discouraging you (with love) in what you do. Listen to them. Weigh their input against your response to the three questions in Step Three. The Body of Christ is designed to help its members. Find a significant person or group of people in your life who will help you understand and confirm your gifts.

5. **Be open to the Holy Spirit surprising you with gifts outside of your normal operating range:** You may have a certain gift mix at one point in your life—down the road it may be different according to how the Holy Spirit directs.

Fold

**SPIRITUAL GIFTS:
ARE THEY FOR
EVERYONE?**

CHECK IT OUT

SKILLS INVENTORY

1. My top three skills

    a. ....

    b. ....

    c. ....

2. Skills I wish I had

    a. ....

    b. ....

    c. ....

(Suggestions: music, computers, athletics, art, photography, counseling, drama, writing, cooking, memory, fixing, designing, etc.)

....

....

....

TEAM EFFORT

WHO AM I?

I was born in .... in ....

                 hospital   **city**

The most influential person in my life is ....

because ....

God has gifted me with the ability to ....

If I knew I couldn't fail, I would ....

SPIRITUAL GIFTS:
ARE THEY FOR
EVERYONE?

 N THE WORD

WHAT ARE THE SPIRITUAL GIFTS?

There are four passages in the New Testament which teach about spiritual gifts. Read the passage of Scripture assigned to your group and write the various gifts under that section. Keep in mind Paul's desire for Christians concerning spiritual gifts. "Now concerning spiritual gifts, brethren, I do not want you to be uninformed" (1 Corinthians 12:1, *RSV*).

Romans 12:6-8	1 Corinthians 12:4-11 1 Corinthians 12:28-30	Ephesians 4:7,8,11,12	1 Peter 4:9-11
1.	1.	1.	1.
2.	2.	2.	2.
3.	3.	3.	3.
4.	4.	4.	
5.	5.	5.	
6.	6.		
7.	7.		
	8.		
	9.		
	10.		
	11.		
	12.		

In God's creative workmanship He designs each person to be remarkably different from all others. As we submit our lives to the Holy Spirit, He also gives a variety of spiritual gifts to each individual. No one person except Jesus Christ has all of the gifts, and at the same time there are *no* ungifted Christians.

Read and summarize 1 Peter 4:10. Explain how your gifts are to be used.

Read 1 Corinthians 12:4-12. Why are there many kinds of spiritual gifts?

How do spiritual gifts benefit others and accomplish God's work?

IN THE WORD

SPIRITUAL GIFTS:
ARE THEY FOR
EVERYONE?

Read 1 Corinthians 12:12-26 and paraphrase Paul's thought.

Here's a helpful guideline to follow when learning about and using your spiritual gifts.

1. Experiment: Sometimes the only way to know if God has gifted you in a certain area is to try out the gift. You will never know if you have the gift of teaching unless you try to teach!

2. Examine your feelings: Your feelings are very important! If you experiment with the gift of teaching and feel extremely uncomfortable and embarrassed, then perhaps you don't have the gift (at this time). On the other hand, if you were to experiment with the gift of hospitality and found that you enjoy entertaining people, sheltering them and feeding needy neighbors and, furthermore, if you receive personal joy, satisfaction and feel used by God in doing these things, then you most likely have the gift of hospitality.

3. Evaluate your effectiveness: Every once in a while stop and think about your effectiveness. Ask yourself these three questions: "Am I effective?" "Am I having a worthwhile impact on these people?" "Is God using me in this particular area?" Remember: God has given everyone a gift that will be effective.

4. Expect confirmation from the Body of Christ: Other Christians should be encouraging or discouraging you (with love) in what you do. Listen to them. Weigh their input against your response to the three questions in Step Three. The Body of Christ is designed to help its members. Find a significant person or group of people in your life who will help you understand and confirm your gifts.

5. Be open to the Holy Spirit surprising you with gifts outside of your normal operating range: You may have a certain gift mix at one point in your life—down the road it may be different according to how the Holy Spirit directs.

So What?

If I could design a specific way to serve God around my giftedness, it might be...

THINGS TO THINK ABOUT

1. What would happen to the Body of Christ if everyone had the same gifts?

2. How can having knowledge about spiritual gifts positively affect a Christian?

3. Why do you think there are so many different types of spiritual gifts within the Body of Christ?

PARENT PAGE

SPIRITUAL GIFTS

"There are different kinds of gifts, but the same Spirit. There are different kinds of service, but the same Lord. There are different kinds of working, but the same God works all of them in all men" (1 Corinthians 12:4-6).

Spiritual gifts that communicate God's Word:
> The gift of evangelism, the gift of prophecy,
> the gift of apostle and missionary

Spiritual gifts that educate God's people:
> The gift of teaching, the gift of exhortation,
> the gift of wisdom, the gift of knowledge

Spiritual gifts that demonstrate God's love:
> The gift of serving, the gift of mercy
> the gift of hospitality, the gift of giving,
> the gift of leadership, the gift of administration,
> the gift of pastoring, the gift of helping

Spiritual gifts that celebrate God's presence:
> The gift of healing, the gift of miracles,
> the gift of tongues, the gift of interpretation of tongues,
> the gift of faith

I'm pretty sure I have the gift of ....

....

I may have the gift of ....

....

I don't think I have the gift of ....

....

Session 1 "Spiritual Gifts: Are They for Everyone?"
Date ....

PARENT PAGE

The spiritual gifts I believe I have are:

1. ....

2. ....

3. ....

I believe I may have these gifts because...

1. ....
....
....

2. ....
....
....

3. ....
....
....

How can understanding our own spiritual gifts help us within our family?

....
....
....
....

Session 1 "Spiritual Gifts: Are They for Everyone?"
Date ....

DISCOVERING THE RIGHT PATH

KEY VERSES

"There are different kinds of working, but the same God works all of them in all men. To one there is given through the Spirit the message of wisdom, to another the message of knowledge by means of the same Spirit." 1 Corinthians 12:6,8

BIBLICAL BASIS

2 Samuel 12:1-14;
Proverbs 2:1-12; 7–9; 13:20;
1 Corinthians 12:6,8;
James 3:17

THE BIG IDEA

The person with the gift of either wisdom or knowledge has the unique ability to uncover insights that might normally be difficult to understand.

AIMS OF THIS SESSION

During this session you will guide students to:
• Examine the spiritual gifts of wisdom and knowledge;
• Discover how these gifts are used within the Body of Christ;
• Implement seeking these gifts and being influenced by those who have these gifts.

CHECK IT OUT

THE GIFT OF WISDOM/THE GIFT OF KNOWLEDGE—
Students rate their aptitudes in the gifts of wisdom and knowledge.

TEAM EFFORT— JUNIOR HIGH/ MIDDLE SCHOOL

CHARACTERISTICS OF A VERY WISE PERSON—
Students list wise traits.

TEAM EFFORT— HIGH SCHOOL

WISDOM TEST—
A checkup on personal wisdom.

IN THE WORD

THE GIFT OF WISDOM/THE GIFT OF KNOWLEDGE—
A Bible study exploring the various aspects of wisdom and knowledge.

THINGS TO THINK ABOUT (OPTIONAL)

Questions to get students thinking and talking about the practical applications of wisdom and knowledge.

PARENT PAGE

A tool to get the session into the home and allow parents and young people to discuss how the gifts of knowledge and wisdom affect the family and the church.

LEADER'S DEVOTIONAL

"He who walks with the wise grows wise, but a companion of fools suffers harm" (Proverbs 13:20).

As a Christian and a youth worker, I don't know what I would have done in countless situations without my youth ministry mentors. When struggling with disillusionment, frustration, confusion, or just needing practical advice on how to help a teenager in need, I've quickly picked up the phone to set up an appointment with someone wiser than myself.

Who is your youth ministry mentor? Who gives you spiritual input and advice? Who listens to you about your struggles and questions? Who do you admire for his or her faithfulness and hungry desire to know God in a deeper, more meaningful way? God has not designed youth ministry to be a solitary, lonely experience. He wants you to walk with the wise so you can grow wise. Coming alongside someone with more life experience, practical knowledge and spiritual insight is just what you and every youth worker needs to persevere in the ministry God has called you to do.

If you don't have a youth ministry mentor, my encouragement to you today is to find one. If you can't find someone who has youth ministry experience, find an older, wiser, knowledgeable brother or sister in Christ who will be in your corner to cheer you on. Many lessons and mistakes can be learned from someone who's walked the road before you. Begin to pray today for God to direct you to someone who can listen, encourage and pray with you. God uses other people in extraordinary, divine ways to give us more wisdom and knowledge. What we learn from our mentors, God will use us to pass on to others. (Written by Joey O'Connor.)

> "Not only are we to ask God for wisdom, but we are to ask in faith. Someone has said, 'Doubt is a non-conductor of grace.' We are not to be double-minded, wanting partly our way and partly God's way."— Millie Stamm

DISCOVERING THE RIGHT PATH

KEY VERSES

"There are different kinds of working, but the same God works all of them in all men. To one there is given through the Spirit the message of wisdom, to another the message of knowledge by means of the same Spirit." 1 Corinthians 12:6,8

BIBLICAL BASIS

2 Samuel 12:1-14; Proverbs 2:1-12; 7-9; 13:20; 1 Corinthians 12:6,8; James 3:17

THE BIG IDEA

The person with the gift of either wisdom or knowledge has the unique ability to uncover insights that might normally be difficult to understand.

CHECK IT OUT (5-10 MINUTES)

THE GIFT OF WISDOM/THE GIFT OF KNOWLEDGE

• Give each student a copy of "The Gift of Wisdom/The Gift of Knowledge" on page 31 and a pen or pencil.

• Have students complete the page.

TEAM EFFORT—JUNIOR HIGH /

MIDDLE SCHOOL (15-20 MINUTES)

CHARACTERISTICS OF A VERY WISE PERSON

• Divide students into groups of three or four.

• Give each group a piece of paper and a pen or pencil.

• Have each group come up with a list of traits of a very wise person. After a few minutes, have each group share their insights.

• Now take a few moments to have students share in their small groups the wisdom traits they see in each other. (This can be a great learning experience as well as an affirmation experience.)

Read verses 7-9. What does God do for those who receive His wisdom?

List the results of allowing wisdom to enter your life according to Proverbs 2:10-12.

                                        Results

(v. 10)   1. _____

           2. _____

(v. 11)   1. _____

           2. _____

(v. 12)   1. _____

           2. _____

Why should you pursue wisdom?

THE GIFT OF KNOWLEDGE

The biblical gift of knowledge has little or nothing to do with your I.Q. The gift of knowledge has been defined as the ability to understand truth that is unknown by natural means.

"To another [is given] the word of knowledge according to the same Spirit" (1 Corinthians 12:8, *NASB*).

Read 2 Samuel 12:1-14. How did Nathan know of David's sin?

What was God's purpose in Nathan's confrontation with David?

How could the gift of knowledge benefit the Body of Christ?

Your church?

SO WHAT?

What specifically can you do to become a person with more wisdom and knowledge of God?

THINGS TO THINK ABOUT (OPTIONAL)

• Use the questions on page 37 after or as a part of "In the Word."

1. How can the gift of wisdom be helpful in dealing with people?

With relationships?

With the church?

2. How can someone with the gift of knowledge be helpful to someone involved in a conflict?

3. What specific ways can you see God using the gift of knowledge in your youth group or family?

PARENT PAGE

• Distribute page to parents.

Fold

T EAM EFFORT—HIGH SCHOOL (15-20 MINUTES)

WISDOM TEST

- Give each student a copy of the "Wisdom Test" on page 33 and a pen or pencil, or display a copy using an overhead projector.
- Have the students complete the page.
- Discuss their answers to the questions.

Here is an interesting discussion starter on the subject of wisdom based on Proverbs 1—9.

1. My friends and family generally consider me to be
   a. a foolish person.
   b. lacking common sense.
   c. a "wise guy."
   d. able to make fairly wise decisions except when it comes to _____.
   e. wiser than most people.
   f. one of the wisest people in the world

2. I consider myself to be
   a. a foolish person.
   b. lacking common sense.
   c. a "wise guy."
   d. able to make fairly wise decisions except when it comes to _____.
   e. wiser then most people.
   f. one of the wisest people in the world

3. I can be talked into things
   a. always or almost always.
   b. often even when I know it is a foolish decision.
   c. only when I really want to be in the first place.
   d. sometimes when I see new information.
   e. only when physical violence accompanies the talk.
   f. never.

4. My wisest actions
   a. have resulted in benefits even others can see.
   b. have brought about changes only I can appreciate.
   c. are still foolish when compared with the actions of most people.
   d. are just about like everyone else's I know.
   e. are wiser than those of anyone else I know.

5. When I'm criticized, I generally
   a. punch out the person who criticized me.
   b. react by screaming and/or yelling.
   c. pout and try to make the person who criticized me feel guilty.
   d. ignore the criticism.
   e. try to honestly evaluate the criticism and change my ways if I feel it is warranted.
   f. appreciate the person who had the guts to share with me and tell him or her so.

6. One area where I generally show wisdom in my life is with
   a. money/finances.
   b. God.

---

   c. friendship.
   d. sex.
   e. family.
   f. use of time/schedule.
   g.
   h. food.

7. One area where I rarely show wisdom and need drastic improvement is with
   a. money/finances
   b. God
   c. friendship
   d. sex
   e. family
   f. use of time/schedule
   g.
   h. food

I N THE WORD (25-30 MINUTES)

THE GIFT OF WISDOM/THE GIFT OF KNOWLEDGE

- Divide students into groups of three or four.
- Give each student a copy of "The Gift of Wisdom/The Gift of Knowledge" on pages 35 and 37 and a pen or pencil, or display a copy using an overhead projector.
- Have students complete the Bible study.

THE GIFT OF WISDOM

Have you ever met a person who was unusually wise? For some reason certain people have the ability to give solid counsel. Their insight into difficult problems is absolutely brilliant. These people probably have the gift of wisdom. Although the Bible challenges all of us to pursue wisdom, there are some people who have an exceptional ability to "see clearly." Their opinions are highly respected.

"For to one is given the word of wisdom through the Spirit" (1 Corinthians 12:8, *NASB*).

James 3:17 draws a picture of godly wisdom. List below the qualities of wisdom given in this verse.

_____

Which of these qualities of wisdom would you most like to work on this week?

_____

What specific steps could you take to develop this quality in your life?

_____

The Book of Proverbs (also called Wisdom Literature) is filled with descriptive illustrations of wisdom. Read Proverbs 2:1-12. Then answer the following questions:

According to verses 1-5, what steps are required before you can gain wisdom?

_____

What significance does verse 6 have in helping you understand wisdom?

_____

Fold

DISCOVERING THE RIGHT PATH

HECK IT OUT

THE GIFT OF WISDOM/THE GIFT OF KNOWLEDGE

The Gift of Wisdom

On a scale of 1-10 rate your responses to these statements:

1	2	3	4	5	6	7	8	9	10
NO		rarely		maybe			sometimes		YES!

.... My friends view me as a person who is wise.

.... I believe God has given me the ability to make wise decisions.

.... God has given me the ability to give clear counsel and advice to others.

.... I feel confident that my decisions are in harmony with God's will.

.... I usually see clear solutions to complicated problems.

.... I believe God has blessed me with the gift of wisdom.

The Gift of Knowledge

On a scale of 1-10 rate your responses to these statements:

1	2	3	4	5	6	7	8	9	10
NO		rarely		maybe			sometimes		YES!

.... I have expressed thoughts of truth that have given insight to others.

.... I desire fully to understand biblical truths.

.... I am able to help others understand God's Word.

.... I tend to use biblical insights when I share with others.

.... I have the ability to learn new insights on my own.

.... I believe I have the gift of knowledge.

**DISCOVERING
THE RIGHT PATH**

TEAM EFFORT

WISDOM TEST[1]

Here is an interesting discussion starter on the subject of wisdom based on Proverbs 7–9.

1. My friends and family generally consider me to be
    a. a foolish person.
    b. lacking common sense.
    c. a "wise guy."
    d. able to make fairly wise decisions except
       when it comes to ....
    e. wiser than most people.
    f. one of the wisest people in the world.

2. I consider myself to be
    a. a foolish person.
    b. lacking common sense.
    c. a "wise guy."
    d. able to make fairly wise decisions except
       when it comes to ....
    e. wiser then most people.
    f. one of the wisest people in the world.

3. I can be talked into things
    a. always or almost always.
    b. often even when I know it is
       a foolish decision.
    c. only when I really want to be in the first place.
    d. sometimes when I see new information.
    e. only when physical violence accompanies the talk.
    f. never.

4. My wisest actions
    a. have resulted in benefits even others can see.
    b. have brought about changes only I can appreciate.
    c. are still foolish when compared with the actions
       of most people.
    d. are just about like everyone else's I know.
    e. are wiser than those of anyone else I know.

5. When I'm criticized, I generally
    a. punch out the person who criticized me.
    b. react by screaming and/or yelling.
    c. pout and try to make the person who
       criticized me feel guilty.
    d. ignore the criticism.
    e. try to honestly evaluate the criticism and
       change my ways if I feel it is warranted.
    f. appreciate the person who had the guts to share
       with me and tell him or her so.

6. One area where I generally show wisdom in my life is with
    a. money/finances.
    b. God.
    c. friendship.
    d. sex.
    e. family.
    f. use of time/schedule.
    g. food.
    h. ....

7. One area where I rarely show wisdom and need drastic improvement is with
    a. money/finances.
    b. God.
    c. friendship.
    d. sex.
    e. family.
    f. use of time/schedule.
    g. food.
    h. ....

Note:

1. *Ideas Number 21-24* (El Cajon, CA:
   Youth Specialties, 1984) pp. 107,108.
   Used by permission.

IN THE WORD

THE GIFT OF WISDOM/THE GIFT OF KNOWLEDGE

The Gift of Wisdom

Have you ever met a person who was unusually wise? For some reason certain people have the ability to give solid counsel. Their insight into difficult problems is absolutely brilliant. These people probably have the gift of wisdom. Although the Bible challenges all of us to pursue wisdom, there are some people who have an exceptional ability to "see clearly." Their opinions are highly respected.

"For to one is given the word of wisdom through the Spirit" (1 Corinthians 12:8, *NASB*).

James 3:17 draws a picture of godly wisdom. List below the qualities of wisdom given in this verse.

Which of these qualities of wisdom would you most like to work on this week?

What specific steps could you take to develop this quality in your life?

The Book of Proverbs (also called wisdom literature) is filled with descriptive illustrations of wisdom. Read Proverbs 2:1-12. Then answer the following questions:

According to verses 1-5 what steps are required before you can gain wisdom?

What significance does verse 6 have in helping you understand wisdom?

Read verses 7-9. What does God do for those who receive His wisdom?

List the results of allowing wisdom to enter your life according to Proverbs 2:10-12.

Results

(v. 10) 1.
2.
(v. 11) 1.
2.
(v. 12) 1.

Why should you pursue wisdom?

 IN THE WORD

DISCOVERING
THE RIGHT PATH

The Gift of Knowledge

The biblical gift of knowledge has little or nothing to do with your I.Q. The gift of knowledge has been defined as the ability to understand truth that is unknown by natural means.

"To another [is given] the word of knowledge according to the same Spirit" (1 Corinthians 12:8, *NASB*).

Read 2 Samuel 12:1-14. How did Nathan know of David's sin?

....

....

What was God's purpose in Nathan's confrontation with David?

....

....

How could the gift of knowledge benefit the Body of Christ?

....

....

Your church?

....

....

SO WHAT?

What specifically can you do to become a person with more wisdom and knowledge for God?

....

....

....

....

....

THINGS TO THINK ABOUT

1. How can the gift of wisdom be helpful in dealing with people?

....

....

With relationships?

....

....

With the church?

....

....

2. How can someone with the gift of knowledge be helpful to someone involved in a conflict?

....

....

3. What specific ways can you see God using the gift of knowledge in your youth group or family?

....

....

DISCOVERING
THE RIGHT PATH

PARENT PAGE

KNOWLEDGE AND WISDOM

A small factory had to stop operations when an essential piece of machinery broke down. When none of the factory personnel could get it operating again, an outside expert took a hammer and gently tapped the machine on a certain spot, and it immediately started running again. When he submitted his bill for $100, the plant supervisor went into a rage and demanded an itemized bill. It read a follows: "For hitting the machine, $1; for knowing where to hit it, $99."

It is essential in the Church today that we have people who "know where to hit it." These people are not necessarily needed to fix machinery, but rather for the important work of making crucial decisions. God may also use people with the gifts of knowledge and wisdom as Christians to research, interpret and investigate His Word so that people may understand it more clearly.

Who do you know who might have this gift?

....

....

....

How have they been a help to you?

....

....

....

What does Proverbs 2:1-12 say about wisdom? Read it together and discuss.

....

....

....

....

Session 2 "Discovering the Right Path"
Date...

ADVENTUROUS FAITH

KEY VERSES

"To one there is given through the Spirit the message of wisdom, to another the message of knowledge by means of the same Spirit, to another faith by the same Spirit, to another gifts of healing by that one Spirit, to another miraculous powers, to another prophecy, to another distinguishing between spirits, to another speaking in different kinds of tongues, and to still another the interpretation of tongues."
1 Corinthians 12:8,9

"It was he who gave some to be apostles, some to be prophets, some to be evangelists, and some to be pastors and teachers." Ephesians 4:11

BIBLICAL BASIS

Proverbs 2:6-8;
Matthew 24:14;
Romans 8:28;
1 Corinthians 12:8,9;
Ephesians 3:1-13; 4:11;
Philippians 1:6;
Hebrews 11:1-40

THE BIG IDEA

The gifts of faith and apostle/missionary requires a person to rely on God when the situation and/or journey seems difficult to believe in.

AIMS OF THIS SESSION

During this session you will guide students to:
• Examine the spiritual gifts of faith, apostleship and missionary;
• Discover the biblical definitions of these important gifts;
• Implement seeking how they can serve God through faith and mission.

CHECK IT OUT

THE GIFT OF FAITH/ THE GIFT OF APOSTLE AND MISSIONARY—
Students rate their aptitudes in the gifts of faith and apostle/missionary.

TEAM EFFORT— JUNIOR HIGH/ MIDDLE SCHOOL

GOD KNOWS WHAT HE IS DOING!—
A story illustrating that God's plans are wiser than man's plans.

TEAM EFFORT— HIGH SCHOOL

FAITH WALK/ FAITH FALL—
A challenge to students' faith in one another.

IN THE WORD

THE GIFT OF FAITH/ THE GIFT OF APOSTLE AND MISSIONARY—
A Bible study exploring the various aspects of faith and apostleship.

THINGS TO THINK ABOUT (OPTIONAL)

Questions to get students thinking and talking about having the faith to do God's will.

PARENT PAGE

A tool to get the session into the home and allow parents and young people to discuss the practical application of faith to their lives.

LEADER'S DEVOTIONAL

"For the LORD gives wisdom, and from his mouth come knowledge and understanding. He holds victory in store for the upright, he is a shield to those whose walk is blameless, for he guards the course of the just and protects the way of his faithful ones" (Proverbs 2:6-8).

While driving home from a rock climbing trip at Joshua Tree National Monument, Paul and I talked about his desire to go to Bible school and become a pastor. I've known Paul for years, but this was the first time he told me of his dream to become a pastor. Paul went through our high school ministry as a student and then served in our college ministry team. His desire to become a pastor really shouldn't have surprised me. Paul, you see, is a rock climber. He has helped countless students up and down high cliffs, roping them up, preparing them for challenges they've never faced before. Paul is a man of faith—a risk-taker. A life of faith, risks and adventure is par for his vertical course in life.

One of my constant prayers during my work with teenagers is for God to raise up new leaders for His church. I've seen that prayer answered in people like Paul. He has a great dream of planting a church. That's a dream that will require great faith, risks and a radical dependence on God. That's a dream worth your time and energy to help young people realize in their lives.

This is the type of lesson where you can instill great challenges of faith and adventure in the hearts of young people. God will use you to plant new visions in open hearts. Who knows…you just may have someone like Paul surprise you someday. It's a risk worth taking. (Written by Joey O'Connor.)

"Many things are possible for the person who has hope. Even more is possible for the person who has faith. And still more is possible for the person who knows how to love. But everything is possible for the person who practices all three virtues."—Brother Lawrence

Tear along perforation. Fold and place this Bible *Tuck-In*™ in your Bible for session use.

S E S S I O N   T H R E E   B I B L E   *T U C K - I N* ™

ADVENTUROUS FAITH

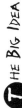 KEY VERSES

"To one there is given through the Spirit the message of wisdom, to another the message of knowledge by means of the same Spirit, to another faith by the same Spirit, to another gifts of healing by that one Spirit, to another miraculous powers, to another prophecy, to another distinguishing between spirits, to another speaking in different kinds of tongues, and to still another the interpretation of tongues." 1 Corinthians 12:8,9

"It was he who gave some to be apostles, some to be prophets, some to be evangelists, and some to be pastors and teachers." Ephesians 4:11

BIBLICAL BASIS

Proverbs 2:6-8; Matthew 24:14; Romans 8:28; 1 Corinthians 12:8,9; Ephesians 3:1-13; 4:11; Philippians 1:6; Hebrews 11:1-40

THE BIG IDEA

The gifts of faith and apostle/missionary requires a person to rely on God when the situation and/or journey seems difficult to believe in.

CHECK IT OUT (5-10 MINUTES)

THE GIFT OF FAITH/THE GIFT OF APOSTLE AND MISSIONARY

• Give each student a copy of "The Gift of Faith/The Gift of Apostle and Missionary" on page 47 and a pen or pencil.

• Have students complete the page.

THE GIFT OF FAITH

On a scale of 1-10 rate your responses to these statements:

1	2	3	4	5	6	7	8	9	10
NO		rarely		maybe		sometimes			YES!

_____ I often feel I know God's will even when others aren't sure.
_____ I enjoy helping others with spiritual needs.
_____ I find it easy to trust in God in difficult situations.
_____ I trust in God for supernatural miracles.
_____ Others in my group see me as a faithful Christian.
_____ I believe I have the gift of faith.

Fold

With the incredible needs in our world, how do you feel about the following statement?
Young men and women should seriously consider becoming missionaries to our hurting world. God needs people who are willing to teach, preach, do business and a host of other things in order for God's message to reach the world.

Mark the boxes that appropriately describe your feelings about the above statement.
☐ I feel guilty.
☐ I'm willing to go if God calls.
☐ I'm not the missionary type.
☐ I'm ready to go today.
I feel _____ about missionary work.
In the space below write out positive and negative reasons for being a missionary.
Positive   Negative

SO WHAT?

If you do not have the gift of apostleship or missionary, what can you do to support the work of Christ around the world?

THINGS TO THINK ABOUT (OPTIONAL)

• Use the questions on page 55 after or as a part of "In the Word."
1. Why is it difficult to have complete faith in God?

2. How would your life be different if you were to have the gift of faith?

3. When you think about going to a different country to spread God's message, what thoughts and feelings come to your mind?

PARENT PAGE

• Distribute page to parents.

THE GIFT OF APOSTLE AND MISSIONARY

On a scale of 1-10 rate your responses to these statements:

1	2	3	4	5	6	7	8	9	10
NO		rarely		maybe		sometimes			YES!

_____ I believe I could learn a new language well enough to minister to those in a different culture.

_____ I feel comfortable when I'm around people of a different culture, race or language.

_____ I adapt easily to a change of settings.

_____ I have a strong desire to see people in other countries won to the Lord.

_____ I am willing to go wherever God wants to send me.

_____ I would like to be a missionary.

TEAM EFFORT—JUNIOR HIGH/
MIDDLE SCHOOL (15-20 MINUTES)

GOD KNOWS WHAT HE IS DOING!

• Give each student a copy of "God Knows What He Is Doing" on page 49 and a pen or pencil, or display a copy using an overhead projector.

• Read the story and then discuss the questions.

1. How did Adam Welch's courageous faith make a difference in the mission field?

2. What plans do you have that must continually be given over to God?

3. Why is it difficult to put our plans and trust in God even with Scriptures like Romans 8:28?

TEAM EFFORT—HIGH SCHOOL (15-20 MINUTES)

FAITH WALK/FAITH FALL

How to do a Faith Walk:

• Divide your students into groups of two.

• Blindfold one student and tell the second student to guide him or her through an obstacle course or trail by spoken directions. With only the words of the guide, the student with the blindfold will have to put his or her faith in the other person.

• Have the students discuss their experience and whether or not they had faith in their leader. Talk about how this relates to their faith in God.

How to do a Faith Fall:

• Divide students into groups of six or eight.

• Have one person at a time in each group stand on something about a foot higher than the ground, fold his or her hands across his or her chest and, by keeping the back straight, he or she is to fall backwards into the group members' hands that are waiting to catch him or her. If this person bends forward, then he or she should do it again. Total faith is when the back is kept straight throughout the fall.

Optional Activity: Interview a Missionary

Another fascinating experience is to interview a missionary (either retired or presently working). Have students ask about some of his or her experiences.

Fold

Some starter questions might be: How receptive were the nationals to the gospel? What are some of the traumatic or dramatic experiences that occurred on the mission field? What did you miss most while living in a different culture? What do you miss about that culture when you return home?

IN THE WORD (25-30 MINUTES)

THE GIFT OF FAITH/THE GIFT OF APOSTLE AND MISSIONARY

THE GIFT OF FAITH

• Divide students into groups of three or four.

• Give each student a copy of "The Gift of Faith/The Gift of Apostle and Missionary" on pages 51, 53 and 55 and a pen or pencil.

• Have students complete the Bible study.

Let's investigate "The Faith Hall of Fame" in the Bible. Read Hebrews 11 together. List each person of faith this chapter mentions and the event associated with his or her great faith.

Why is this such an inspiring chapter?

Define the word "faith" in your own words using Hebrews 11:1 as a resource.

What eternal truth is found in Hebrews 11:6?

Do you know any modern-day people who could be included in "The Faith Hall of Fame"?

Create a list alongside your Bible "Hall of Famers."

Why is it difficult at times to have faith?

What could you accomplish with your life if you had more faith?

THE GIFT OF APOSTLE AND MISSIONARY

Paul was an apostle and missionary. Read Ephesians 3:1-13. What was Paul trying to communicate to the Gentiles (see v. 6)?

What title did Paul give himself (see v. 7)?

Because of his title, what was Paul able to do (see v. 8)?

What was the goal of his missionary work (see vv. 9-12)?

From what you know of Paul, did he accomplish this goal?

What is the meaning of Jesus' statement in Matthew 24:14?

ADVENTUROUS
FAITH

CHECK IT OUT

THE GIFT OF FAITH/THE GIFT OF APOSTLE AND MISSIONARY

The Gift of Faith

On a scale of 1-10 rate your responses to these statements:

1	2	3	4	5	6	7	8	9	10
NO		rarely		maybe			sometimes		YES!

.... I often feel I know God's will even when others aren't sure.

.... I enjoy helping others with spiritual needs.

.... I find it easy to trust in God in difficult situations.

.... I trust in God for supernatural miracles.

Others in my group see me as a faithful Christian.

I believe I have the gift of faith.

The Gift of Apostle and Missionary

On a scale of 1-10 rate your responses to these statements:

1	2	3	4	5	6	7	8	9	10
NO		rarely		maybe			sometimes		YES!

.... I believe I could learn a new language well enough to minister to those in a different culture.

.... I feel comfortable when I'm around people of a different culture, race or language.

.... I adapt easily to a change of settings.

.... I have a strong desire to see people in other countries won to the Lord.

.... I am willing to go wherever God wants to send me.

.... I would like to be a missionary.

**ADVENTUROUS
FAITH**

GOD KNOWS WHAT HE IS DOING!

"And we know that in all things God works for the good of those who love him, who have been called according to his purpose" (Romans 8:28).

From a very young age Adam Welch had a strong desire to become a missionary for Jesus Christ. One of the greatest days of his life was the day he was accepted to become a missionary to Africa. Unfortunately his dream was short-lived when it was found that because of medical reasons, he would not be able to go on the mission field.

He was heartbroken, but he prayerfully returned home. God gave him a new vision. He would create a business enterprise that would make millions of dollars, enabling Adam Welch to support hundreds of missionaries all over the world.

Adam Welch worked hard and created the Welch's Grape Juice Company. God has used him to give literally millions of dollars to the work of missions. In hindsight, more was done for the Kingdom of God through Adam Welch staying at home than one man going to the mission field.

God's plans are not always our plans, for his plans carry an even greater purpose.

1. How did Adam Welch's courageous faith make a difference in the mission field?

....

....

2. What plans do you have that must continually be given over to God?

....

....

3. Why is it difficult to put our plans and trust in God even with Scriptures like Romans 8:28?

....

....

....

ADVENTUROUS
FAITH

THE GIFT OF FAITH/THE GIFT OF APOSTLE AND MISSIONARY

The Gift of Faith

"To one is given...faith by the same Spirit" (1 Corinthians 12:8,9 *RSV*).

Have you ever met a person with extraordinary faith? Their gift of faith causes them to trust in God beyond their remarkably established, risk-taking faith for exceptional miracles. All Christians are believers by faith; yet there are those who, from the Bible days to the present day, have demonstrated an unusual ability to depend on God.

Let's investigate "The Faith Hall of Fame" in the Bible. Read Hebrews 11 together. List each person of faith this chapter mentions and the event associated with his or her great faith.

Why is this such an inspiring chapter?

Define the word "faith" in your own words using Hebrews 11:1 as a resource.

What eternal truth is found in Hebrews 11:6?

Do you know any modern-day people who could be included in "The Faith Hall of Fame"?

Create a list alongside your Bible "Hall of Famers."

Why is it difficult at times to have faith?

What could you accomplish with your life if you had more faith?

IN THE WORD

ADVENTUROUS
FAITH

The Gift of Apostle and Missionary[1]

"His gifts were that some should be apostles" (Ephesians 4:11, *RSV*).

To best understand the meaning of apostleship we must look at the first apostles. They were the commissioned "messengers" of the early church. The apostle took the message of the Good News of Jesus Christ to the world. In many ways they led the way for new territory to be charted for Christ. A modern-day apostle is one who feels God's call to take the same message of Jesus Christ to the world. Many people today who have the gift of apostleship are missionaries.

Paul was an apostle and missionary. Read Ephesians 3:1-13. What was Paul trying to communicate to the Gentiles? (see v. 6)

....

....

....

What title did Paul give himself (see v. 7)?

....

....

Because of his title, what was Paul able to do (see v. 8)?

....

....

....

What was the goal of his missionary work (see vv. 9-12)?

....

....

....

From what you know of Paul, did he accomplish this goal?

....

....

....

What is the meaning of Jesus' statement in Matthew 24:14?

....

....

....

ADVENTUROUS FAITH

 **IN THE WORD**

With the incredible needs in our world how do you feel about the following statement?
Young men and women should seriously consider becoming missionaries to our hurting world. God needs people who are willing to teach, preach, do business and a host of other things in order for God's message to reach the world.

Mark the boxes that describe appropriately your feelings about the above statement.
- ❏ I feel guilty.
- ❏ I'm willing to go if God calls.
- ❏ I'm not the missionary type.
- ❏ I'm ready to go today.

I feel _____ about missionary work.

In the space below write out positive and negative reasons for being a missionary.

Positive	**Negative**

SO WHAT?

If you do not have the gift of apostleship or missionary, what can you do to support the work of Christ around the world?

1. Most scholars would say these are two separate gifts (apostle and missionary) yet they are in the "same gift mix." We have chosen to combine them for the sake of simplicity.

 **THINGS TO THINK ABOUT**

1. Why is it difficult to have complete faith in God?

2. How would your life be different if you were to have the gift of faith?

3. When you think about going to a different country to spread God's message, what thoughts and feelings come to your mind?

PARENT PAGE

ADVENTUROUS
FAITH

ORDINARY PEOPLE DOING EXTRAORDINARY THINGS FOR GOD

"Now faith is being sure of what we hope for and certain of what we do not see. This is what the ancients were commended for. And without faith it is impossible to please God, because anyone who comes to him must believe that he exists and that he rewards those who earnestly seek him" (Hebrews 11:1,2,6).

Faith is...ordinary people doing extraordinary things with their lives for God.

Faith is...Bob Wieland walking across America on his hands because he has no feet!

Faith is...Dave and Natalie Hess becoming undercover missionaries in a country where it's illegal to be a Christian.

Faith is...Rachel deciding to *not* abort her child even though her boyfriend is pressing her to abort.

Faith is...Ted choosing to *not* cheat on an exam and get a poor grade even though he couldn't get caught.

As a family fill in a few of these blanks:

Faith is...

....

....

Faith is...

....

....

Faith is...

....

....

Now answer these questions.

1. **What are you doing right now that you couldn't do without the supernatural help of God?**

....

....

2. **What areas of your life could use a real "faith lift"?**

....

....

3. **When it comes to being a person with a strong faith in God,**
   ❏ I feel very weak.
   ❏ I keep trying.
   ❏ I know God is using me.

"Being confident of this, that he who began a good work in you will carry it on to completion until the day of Christ Jesus" (Philippians 1:6).

What is God saying to you in this verse?

....

....

....

Session 3 "Adventurous Faith"
Date..

EXPERIENCING GOD'S LOVE

Key Verses

"To another faith by the same Spirit, to another gifts of healing by that one Spirit, to another miraculous powers, to another prophecy, to another distinguishing between spirits, to another speaking in different kinds of tongues, and to still another the interpretation of tongues."
1 Corinthians 12:9,10

Biblical Basis

1 Kings 18:1-45;
Psalm 77:14;
Matthew 9:35; 12:38-40; 13:14,15;
Luke 4:18;
Acts 2; 3:2-8; 8:6-8; 10:44-46;
14:8-10; 19:1-7;
1 Corinthians 12:8-10;
14:2,4,5,9,13-19,22,26-28,33,40;
James 5:14-16;
1 Peter 2:24

The Big Idea

Sometimes God uses signs and wonders to demonstrate His love and presence in the world. Our God is a God of miracles.

Aims of This Session

During this session you will guide students to:

- Examine the spiritual gifts of miracles, healing and tongues;
- Discover what the Bible has to say about signs and wonders;
- Implement lifestyles of seeking and searching for all God has for His people.

Check It Out

THE GIFTS OF MIRACLES AND HEALING/THE GIFT OF TONGUES—

Students rate their aptitudes in the gifts of miracles, healing and tongues.

Team Effort— Junior High/ Middle School

A MIRACULOUS ROLE-PLAY—

Students enact the story of Elijah and the prophets of Baal.

Team Effort— High School

MIRACLES—

An investigation of miraculous healings.

In the Word

THE GIFTS OF TONGUES AND THE INTERPRETATION OF TONGUES/THE GIFT OF HEALING—

A Bible study on the various aspects of the sign gifts.

Things to Think About (OPTIONAL)

Questions to get students thinking and talking about the purpose and use of the sign gifts.

Parent Page

A tool to get the session into the home and allow parents and young people to discuss the significance of miracles.

Leader's Devotional

"You are the God who performs miracles; you display your power among the peoples" (Psalm 77:14).

I have never seen a blind man healed of his blindness, I have never seen a lame man walk and I've never seen a dead person be raised from the dead, but I still believe in miracles. I still believe in the God who performs miracles. Why? Because I've seen tons of miracles happen in teenagers' lives.

Being a youth worker provides all sorts of opportunities to see our awesome God at work. Youth ministry is fertile ground to see the miracles of God take root in the lives of teenagers. It's just that we often forget what miracles really are. How about when a fifteen-year-old receives Christ for the first time? Isn't that a miracle? What about when a young person overcomes dependency on drugs and alcohol? Isn't that a miracle? What about when a teenager learns to love the parents he used to hate? *Now that's a miracle!*

Miracles are all around us, but I think we've lost our desire to search for signs of God at work in people's lives. Do you still believe in miracles? Do you look for God to demonstrate Himself in amazing and incredible ways?

Miracles are testimonies to the power of God designed to draw us closer to Him. Too often, Christians get split along denominational lines over what constitutes a miracle or what signs and wonders God still performs today. God wants every miracle He performs to bring you closer to Him. Perhaps this lesson will be a reminder to keep looking for signs and wonders in the lives of young people. Young people want to believe in an all-powerful God. Our God is a God of miracles and He uses youth workers like you to show teenagers that both He and miracles still exist. (Written by Joey O'Connor.)

"Let no one therefore say that our Lord Jesus Christ doeth not those things now, and on this account prefer the former to the present ages of the Church... The Lord did those things to invite us to the faith."— St. Augustine

Tear along perforation. Fold and place this Bible Tuck-In™ in your Bible for session use.

EXPERIENCING GOD'S LOVE

······· Fold ·······

 KEY VERSES

"To another faith by the same Spirit, to another gifts of healing by that one Spirit, to another miraculous powers, to another prophecy, to another distinguishing between spirits, to another speaking in different kinds of tongues, and to still another the interpretation of tongues."
1 Corinthians 12:9,10

B IBLICAL BASIS

1 Kings 18:1-45; Psalm 77:14; Matthew 9:35; 12:38-40; 13:14,15; Luke 4:18; Acts 2: 3:2-8; 8:6-8; 10:44-46; 14:8-10; 19:1-7; 1 Corinthians 12:8-10; 14:2,4,5,9,13-19,22,26-28,33,40; James 5:14-16; 1 Peter 2:24

T HE BIG IDEA

Sometimes God uses signs and wonders to demonstrate His love and presence in the world. Our God is a God of miracles.

C HECK IT OUT (5-10 MINUTES)

• Give each student a copy of "The Gifts of Miracles and Healing/The Gift of Tongues" on page 63 and a pen or pencil.
• Have students complete the page.

THE GIFTS OF MIRACLES AND HEALING/THE GIFT OF TONGUES

THE GIFTS OF MIRACLES AND HEALING

On a scale of 1-10 rate your responses to these statements:

1	2	3	4	5	6	7	8	9	10
NO		rarely		maybe		sometimes			YES!

_____ God has used me in a supernatural way to heal someone.
_____ I have healed a handicapped person.
_____ Many incredible acts of God have happened to others through me.
_____ I have the ability to heal.
_____ God is glorified when He heals others through me.
_____ I believe I have the gift of miracles/healing.

THE GIFT OF HEALING

Matthew 9:35 ....
Acts 3:2-8 ....
Acts 8:6-8 ....
Acts 14:8-10 ....

List the steps given in James 5:14-16 for healing the sick.

Let's look at another type of healing—emotional healing.

"The Spirit of the Lord is upon me, because he hath anointed me to preach the gospel to the poor; he hath sent me to heal the broken-hearted, to preach deliverance to the captives, and recovering of sight to the blind, to set at liberty them that are bruised" (Luke 4:18, KJV).

The word translated "broken-hearted" refers to those who are emotionally and mentally shattered. In fact, the last phrase of this quotation, "to set at liberty them that are bruised" also refers to emotional healing.

Could it be possible that emotional healing might be as important to our understanding of healing as physical healing? Why or why not?

What occupations are aimed at providing emotional healing?

How might the gift of healing be demonstrated by people who practice these occupations?

In the Bible there is another form of healing called spiritual healing.

Read Matthew 13:14,15. How could the prophecy from Isaiah refer to spiritual healing?

Read this statement found in 1 Peter 2:24, "Christ himself carried our sins on his body to the cross, so that we might die to sin and live for righteousness. By his wounds you have been healed" (TEV). According to this verse, why are we healed?

How does this verse relate to your life?

In light of this information on physical, emotional and spiritual healing, what do you perceive to be the definition of healing? Share it with your group.

SO WHAT?

Whether or not you have the gift of healing, what can you be doing to help heal people with physical, emotional and spiritual needs?

Complete this sentence. I may not have the God-given gift of healing, but I can attempt to heal others by...

T HINGS TO THINK ABOUT (OPTIONAL)

• Use the questions on page 75 after or as a part of "In the Word."
1. Do the gifts of healing, tongues, and miracles have a place in the church today?

Why or why not?

2. How does healing benefit the Body of Christ? Is a doctor as much of a healer as a "faith healer"?

3. What is one miracle that God has done in your life in the past year?

P ARENT PAGE

• Distribute page to parents.

On a scale of 1-10 rate your responses to these statements:

1   2   3   4   5   6   7   8   9   10
NO   rarely   maybe   sometimes   YES!

_____ I believe I have a prayer language which is in a tongue unknown to me.
_____ I have spoken in tongues.
_____ When I speak in tongues, I feel God's Spirit within me.
_____ Others have interpreted my unknown prayer language.
_____ An unknown language comes to me when I'm at a loss for words in my prayer time.
_____ I believe I have the gift of tongues.

TEAM EFFORT—JUNIOR HIGH/ MIDDLE SCHOOL (15-20 Minutes)

A MIRACULOUS ROLE-PLAY: ELIJAH MEETS THE PROPHETS OF BAAL (1 KINGS 18:1-45)

• Choose a few students before the meeting or the prior week to act out the incredible story of Elijah and the Prophets of Baal. (The longer the preparation notice the better this role-play can become.) You can guide the students or better yet let their imagination run wild. (It will!) Give them the Scripture. The Living Bible has an interesting version in easy modern day English. First Kings 18:1-6 and 40-45 can be told by a narrator if you wish.

• After the students act out the story, here are some possible discussion questions:
1. What are the miracles in this story?
2. How was God glorified?
3. What positive results took place?
4. What lessons can we learn from this story?

TEAM EFFORT—HIGH SCHOOL (15-20 Minutes)

MIRACLES

• Divide students into groups of three or four.
• Give each student a copy of "Miracles" on page 65 and a pen or pencil, or display a copy using an overhead projector.
• Have students complete the page.
Read Acts 3:1-12. Who was healed in this story?
By what power was this man healed?
Why were the people who saw the miracle amazed?

Why was Peter upset by their amazement?

Why do you think God uses miracles?

What are some modern-day miracles?

IN THE WORD (25-30 Minutes)

THE GIFT OF TONGUES AND THE INTERPRETATION OF TONGUES/ THE GIFT OF HEALING

• Divide students into groups of three or four.
• Give each student a copy of "In the Word" pages 67, 69, 71 and 73 a pen or pencil.
• Have students complete the Bible study.

THE GIFT OF TONGUES AND THE INTERPRETATION OF TONGUES
What is the gift of tongues?

It is evident that in the early church many men and women spoke in tongues. Read the following verses and summarize your impression of these Scripture references.

Acts 2:1-13 _____
Acts 10:44-46 _____
Acts 19:1-7 _____
Read 1 Corinthians 14:2. What do you think is the significance of this verse?

What is the purpose of the gift of tongues?

Let's look at three purposes given in the New Testament.
1. A Sign
Read Acts 2 and 1 Corinthians 14:22. To whom is the sign directed?

What is the purpose of the sign?

2. Edification (building up the Body of Christ)
Read 1 Corinthians 14:4. Who is edified?

Read 1 Corinthians 14:5. Who is edified when speaking in tongues is interpreted? (Also see v. 14:26.)

Read 1 Corinthians 14:13-19 and summarize what this Scripture teaches about the gift of tongues and the interpretation of tongues.

3. Prayer
Read 1 Corinthians 14:4. Do you think speaking in tongues is a form of prayer?

What Are the Biblical Guidelines?

Paul gave the church at Corinth instructions for speaking in tongues. He wanted to make it quite clear that the gift of tongues was no greater than the other gifts of the Spirit.
Read 1 Corinthians 14:26-28,33,40. List Paul's rules:
(v. 26) 1. _____   (vv. 27,28) 3. _____
(v. 27) 2. _____   (vv. 33,40) 4. _____

From what you have learned, what are your present thoughts about speaking in tongues?

EXPERIENCING
GOD'S LOVE

HECK IT OUT

THE GIFTS OF MIRACLES AND HEALING, AND THE GIFT OF TONGUES

The Gifts of Miracles and Healing

On a scale of 1-10 rate your responses to these statements:

1	2	3	4	5	6	7	8	9	10
NO		rarely		maybe			sometimes		YES!

.... God has used me in a supernatural way to heal someone.

.... I have healed a handicapped person.

.... Many incredible acts of God have happened to others through me.

.... I have the ability to heal.

.... God is glorified when He heals others through me.

.... I believe I have the gift of miracles/healing.

The Gift of Tongues

On a scale of 1-10 rate your responses to these statements:

1	2	3	4	5	6	7	8	9	10
NO		rarely		maybe			sometimes		YES!

.... I believe I have a prayer language which is in a tongue unknown to me.

.... I have spoken in tongues.

.... When I speak in tongues, I feel God's Spirit within me.

.... Others have interpreted my unknown prayer language.

.... An unknown language comes to me when I'm at a loss for words in my prayer time.

.... I believe I have the gift of tongues.

EXPERIENCING
GOD'S LOVE

⬤ TEAM EFFORT

MIRACLES

Scattered throughout the Bible are incredible illustrations of miracles: the parting of the Red Sea for Moses and the people of Israel, Elijah breathing life into the widow's dead son, Jesus turning water into wine, Jesus walking on water, and more. Sometimes the miracles of the Bible seem distant when we look at them from the 20th century. Let's investigate this gift to see if it is for today.

"There are different kinds of spiritual gifts...to another miraculous powers" (1 Corinthians 12:4,10).

Read Acts 3:1-12. Who was healed in this story?

_____

_____

By what power was this man healed?

_____

_____

Why were the people who saw the miracle amazed?

_____

_____

Why was Peter upset by their amazement?

_____

_____

Why do you think God uses miracles?

_____

_____

What are some modern-day miracles?

_____

_____

IN THE WORD

THE GIFTS OF TONGUES AND THE INTERPRETATION OF TONGUES/THE GIFT OF HEALING

The Gift of Tongues and the Interpretation of Tongues

"To one there is given through the Spirit…speaking in different kinds of tongues, and to still another the interpretation of tongues" (1 Corinthians 12:8,10).

In the Christian faith, speaking in tongues and the interpretation of tongues are perhaps the most widely debated and misunderstood gifts of the Spirit. Some say speaking in tongues is not a gift, others say it is a gift. Some say the gift was only for the first-century Church; others believe tongues to be evidence of the baptism of the Holy Spirit. Let's investigate what the Bible has to say about this interesting gift so we can begin to develop our own biblical opinion on the subject.[1]

What is the gift of tongues?

It is evident that in the early church many men and women spoke in tongues. Read the following verses and summarize your impression of these Scripture references.

Acts 2:1-13

Acts 10:44-46

Acts 19:1-7

Read 1 Corinthians 14:2. What do you think is the significance of this verse?

What is the purpose of the gift of tongues?

Let's look at three purposes given in the New Testament.
1. A Sign

Read Acts 2 and 1 Corinthians 14:22. To whom is the sign directed?

What is the purpose of the sign?

IN THE WORD

2. Edification (building up the Body of Christ)

Read 1 Corinthians 14:4. Who is edified?

....

Read 1 Corinthians 14:5. Who is edified when speaking in tongues is interpreted? (Also, see v. 14:26.)

....

Read 1 Corinthians 14:13-19 and summarize what this Scripture teaches about the gift of tongues and the interpretation of tongues.

....

3. Prayer

Read 1 Corinthians 14:4. Do you think speaking in tongues is a form of prayer?

....

....

What *Are* the Biblical Guidelines?
Paul gave the church at Corinth instructions for speaking in tongues. He wanted to make it quite clear that the gift of tongues was no greater than the other gifts of the Spirit.
Read 1 Corinthians 14:26-28,33,40. List Paul's rules:

(v. 26)   1. ....

(v. 27)   2. ....

(vv. 27,28) 3. ....

(vv. 33,40) 4. ....

From what you have learned, what are your present thoughts about speaking in tongues?

....

....

IN THE WORD

EXPERIENCING
GOD'S LOVE

The Gift of Healing

"There are different kinds of gifts, but the same Spirit...to another gifts of healing by that one Spirit" (1 Corinthians 12:4,9).

At one time or another we have all prayed for healing, either for ourselves or for a loved one. We've heard of miraculous healings and we've also known times when it was apparent that God did not answer our prayer for a healing. Yet the Bible does speak of the gift of healing, and the Gospels and the Book of Acts are filled with miraculous healings from God.

Read the verses below and write down the person who had the gift of healing and what or who they healed. (This is not a complete list.)

Matthew 9:35 ....

Acts 3:2-8 ....

Acts 8:6-8 ....

Acts 14:8-10 ....

List the steps given in James 5:14-16 for healing the sick.

....

....

Let's look at another type of healing—emotional healing.

"The Spirit of the Lord is upon me, because he hath anointed me to preach the gospel to the poor; he hath sent me to heal the broken-hearted, to preach deliverance to the captives, and recovering of sight to the blind, to set at liberty them that are bruised" (Luke 4:18, *KJV*).

The word translated "broken-hearted" refers to those who are emotionally and mentally shattered. In fact, the last phrase of this quotation, "to set at liberty them that are bruised" also refers to emotional healing.

Could it be possible that emotional healing might be as important to our understanding of healing as physical healing? Why or why not?

....

....

What occupations are aimed at providing emotional healing?

....

....

How might the gift of healing be demonstrated in people who practice these occupations?

....

....

EXPERIENCING GOD'S LOVE

 N THE WORD

In the Bible there is another form of healing called spiritual healing.

Read Matthew 13:14,15. How could the prophecy from Isaiah refer to spiritual healing?

Read this statement found in 1 Peter 2:24. "Christ himself carried our sins on his body to the cross, so that we might die to sin and live for righteousness. By his wounds you have been healed" (*TEV*). According to this verse, why are we healed?

How does this verse relate to your life?

In light of this information on physical, emotional and spiritual healing, what do you perceive to be the definition of healing? Share it with your group.

SO WHAT?

Whether or not you have the gift of healing, what can you be doing to help heal people with physical, emotional and spiritual needs?

Complete this sentence. I may not have the God-given gift of healing, but I can attempt to heal others by...

Note:

1. Please note that in the limited space available we cannot attempt to provide a thorough study of these gifts.

⬤ Things to Think About

1. Do the gifts of healing, tongues and miracles have a place in the church today?

   ....

   Why or why not?

   ....

   ....

   ....

2. How does healing benefit the Body of Christ? Is a doctor as much of a healer as a "faith healer"?

   ....

   ....

   ....

3. What is one miracle that God has done in your life in the past year?

   ....

   ....

   ....

PARENT PAGE

MIRACLES

Read Matthew 12:38. What did the Pharisees want?

_____

_____

Read Matthew 12:39,40. How did Christ respond?

_____

_____

Does this mean we should never ask for miracles?

_____

_____

What miracles, if any, have taken place in your own life?

_____

_____

What miracles would you like to take place in your life?

_____

_____

In your family?

_____

_____

Session 4 "Experiencing God's Love"
Date _____

Unit II

SPIRITUAL GIFTS THAT COME ALONGSIDE GOD'S PEOPLE

Leonard Bernstein, the famous orchestra conductor, was asked, "What is the most difficult instrument to play?" He responded: "Second fiddle. I can get plenty of first violinists, but to find one who plays second violin with as much enthusiasm, or second French horn or second flute, now that's a problem. And yet if no one plays second, we have no harmony."

We don't think the church has done a good enough job helping students understand that the "come alongside" gifts are just as important to the life of the church as the "up-front" gifts. It's very exciting for the kid in your group who is an incredible encourager but not a very good teacher of the Word to see that he/she is also grace gifted. These come alongside gifts are the backbone of the church. Many who have this gift mix do not receive the pats on the back or the words of encouragement that they should from church leadership. That is about to change! We hope you will encourage like crazy your kids who have some of these serving gifts. They are the backbone of the Lord's ministry on planet Earth.

ENCOURAGING GOD'S PEOPLE

KEY VERSE

"But encourage one another daily, as long as it is called Today, so that none of you may be hardened by sin's deceitfulness." Hebrews 3:13

BIBLICAL BASIS

Acts 4:36; 9:27; 11:19-26; 13; 14:21,22; 15:36-41; 20:17-35; 2 Thessalonians 2:16,17; Hebrews 3:13; 10:25

THE BIG IDEA

Exhortation is the unique ability to freely encourage as well as confront other people in order to lead them in the right direction.

AIMS OF THIS SESSION

During this session you will guide students to:
• Examine the spiritual gift of exhortation;
• Discover the importance and value of encouraging one another;
• Implement lifestyles of encouragement.

CHECK IT OUT

THE GIFT OF EXHORTATION—

Students rate their aptitudes in the gift of exhortation.

TEAM EFFORT— JUNIOR HIGH/ MIDDLE SCHOOL

WEIRD PEOPLE TRICKS—

An opportunity to spotlight unusual talents.

TEAM EFFORT— HIGH SCHOOL

AN ENCOURAGING WORD—

An activity to practice giving encouragement.

IN THE WORD

THE GIFT OF EXHORTATION—

A Bible study exploring the various aspects of encouragement.

THINGS TO THINK ABOUT (OPTIONAL)

Questions to get the students thinking and talking about how to apply the gift of exhortation.

PARENT PAGE

A tool to get the session into the home and allow parents and young people to practice encouraging one another.

Leader's Devotional

May our Lord Jesus Christ himself and God our Father, who loved us and by his grace gave us eternal encouragement and good hope, encourage your hearts and strengthen you in every good deed and word" (2 Thessalonians 2:16,17).

In the bottom drawer of the blue file cabinet that sits next to my desk, I have a whole file filled with scraps of paper, scrawled notes, greeting cards, personal stationery and note-book paper. *All letters of encouragement and thanks.* This isn't a "How Great I Am" file, but a file full of thanksgiving and honest appreciation. It's the type of file every youth worker needs to encourage him or her when life and ministry look hopeless.

In your work with teenagers, who is your encourager? Who is your Barnabas? Discouragement is one of the major diseases of youth ministry. It's so easy for a youth worker to be discouraged by "getting dissed" with…

•Disrespect: You spent three hours working on a talk and when you try to deliver it, nobody is listening. They're all talking and joking around.

•Disappointment: You hear rumors that one of your key leadership students is making some big-time mistakes and when you try to talk to him, he flat out lies to your face. What do you do—call him a liar?

•Disinterest: Your youth ministry borders on the double-edged razor of apathy and boredom. You've tried everything, but you're now ready to give up.

•Disillusion: You thought youth ministry would be fun and exciting, but you're seeing no evidence of teenagers walking closer with God.

The devil would love to do you in with discouragement. Today, the Holy Spirit wants to empower you with encouragement. Let this lesson be an affirmation of His work in your life and a reminder that He's still in control. (Written by Joey O'Connor.)

"All of us need encouragement—somebody to believe in us. To reassure and reinforce us. To help us pick up the pieces and go on. To provide us with increased determination in spite of the odds."— Charles Swindoll

ENCOURAGING GOD'S PEOPLE

K EY VERSES

"But encourage one another daily, as long as it is called Today, so that none of you may be hardened by sin's deceitfulness." Hebrews 3:13

B IBLICAL BASIS

Acts 4:36; 9:27; 11:19-26; 13; 14:21,22; 15:36-41; 20:17-35; 2 Thessalonians 2:16,17; Hebrews 3:13; 10:25

T HE BIG IDEA

Exhortation is the unique ability to freely encourage as well as confront other people in order to lead them in the right direction.

C HECK IT OUT (5-10 MINUTES)

THE GIFT OF EXHORTATION

• Give each student a copy of "The Gift of Exhortation" on page 85 and a pen or pencil.
• Have students complete the page.

On a scale of 1-10 rate your responses to these statements:

1	2	3	4	5	6	7	8	9	10
NO		rarely		maybe		sometimes			YES!

_____ I am known for the way I encourage others.
_____ I believe I have the ability to comfort those who are "off track" and help them get back on track.
_____ I have a desire to learn more about counseling so I can help others.
_____ I have helped others in their struggles.
_____ I believe I have the gift of encouragement.

T EAM EFFORT—JUNIOR HIGH/

MIDDLE SCHOOL (15-20 MINUTES)

WEIRD PEOPLE TRICKS

• Every youth group has at least two students who can do something that is really weird. These are the things that you try to discourage during your meetings. Well, here's your

---

Fold

T HINGS TO THINK ABOUT (OPTIONAL)

• Use the questions on page 91 after or as a part of "In the Word."

1. Why is it sometimes difficult to encourage others?

2. The gift of exhortation involves encouragement and sometimes confrontation. Why is it difficult to confront someone even though you know it will help him or her get back on the right path?

3. The word exhortation means "to come alongside." After all that you have learned about encouragement, what do you think this will come to mean in your own life?

P ARENT PAGE

• Distribute page to parents.

chance to let those students shine. Make a competition out of it. At the end of the competition, let the group vote on their favorite.

• Interview the budding performers to find out how it felt to be applauded for doing something weird. Make the point: Now can you imagine how good it will feel when we are applauded for doing something good? That's encouragement!

• For more participation, announce this experience the week before you do it in youth group.

TEAM EFFORT—HIGH SCHOOL (15-20 MINUTES)

AN ENCOURAGING WORD

• Find 3-5 students to sit on a panel and share a difficult burden with the youth group. Make sure you use students who feel comfortable sharing a struggle. (If your kids feel uncomfortable, use adult leaders.)

• After each student shares their issue(s), let the group ask clarification questions if needed. Then have the members in the group give the students encouraging words about their problem.

• Optional: Interview the panel members, asking them how it felt to be encouraged.

IN THE WORD (25-30 MINUTES)

THE GIFT OF EXHORTATION

• Divide students into groups of three or four.

• Give each student a copy of "The Gift of Exhortation" on page 87 and a pen or pencil, display a copy using an overhead projector.

• Have students complete the Bible study.

You've probably been around people who have a real gift for encouraging others. They have the unique ability to make you feel special. Their ministry of comfort, challenge and counsel helps and heals discouraged people.

The word exhortation means "to come alongside." Exhorting someone is coming alongside that person for the sake of encouraging and advising him or her.

Do you know someone who has the gift of exhortation? Who?

What are the qualities or characteristics that help you to see that he or she has this special gift?

The apostle Paul had the gift of exhortation. As you read the Book of Acts you will see that Paul was an encouragement to others even after enduring brutal beatings, mobs and imprisonment.

How did Paul use his gift of exhortation in these Scripture passages?

Acts 14:21,22

Acts 20:17-35

Another New Testament Christian who stands out as possessing the gift of exhortation is Barnabas. Everywhere

---

Barnabas appears in the Bible, he is encouraging someone.

According to Acts 4:36, what does the name Barnabas mean?

Read Acts 11:19-26. List several ways Barnabas was an encouragement to the believers in Antioch.

How was Barnabas an encouragement to Paul in Acts 9:27?

You might need to read the entire account of Paul's conversion in chapter nine for a clearer understanding. Barnabas and Paul left the church in Antioch and began to preach around the world (see Acts 13). On their first long trip, Barnabas wanted to take his nephew John (called Mark) who Barnabas saw as a potential Christian leader. (Barnabas and encouraged potential in people.) John Mark didn't make it through the entire trip and left to return to Jerusalem (see Acts 13:13). After the first trip was completed, Paul and Barnabas decided to go back to visit the places they had been (see Acts 15:36). Again Barnabas wanted to take John Mark, but Paul insisted they shouldn't take him since he deserted them earlier. A sharp disagreement broke out. Paul thought of the work; Barnabas thought of the man (see Acts 15:37-41).

Read Acts 15:36-41. What was the result of the argument (see vv. 39,40)?

If you were Paul, would you have given John Mark a second chance? Why or why not?

What characteristics made Barnabas a good friend?

We might be missing half of the New Testament books had Barnabas not used his gift of encouragement. Although Barnabas never wrote a book in the New Testament, Paul wrote 13 and Mark wrote one—and Barnabas encouraged them both!

SO WHAT?

Who in your life needs your encouragement?

Encouragement One

Encouragement Two

Encouragement Three

What specifically will you do to encourage them?

Encouragement One

Encouragement Two

Encouragement Three

Fold

ENCOURAGING
GOD'S PEOPLE

 HECK IT OUT

THE GIFT OF EXHORTATION

On a scale of 1-10 rate your responses to these statements:

1	2	3	4	5	6	7	8	9	10
NO		rarely		maybe			sometimes		YES!

.... I am known for the way I encourage others.

.... I believe I have the ability to comfort those who are "off track" and help them get back on track.

.... I have a desire to learn more about counseling so I can help others.

.... I have helped others in their struggles.

.... I believe I have the gift of encouragement.

ENCOURAGING
GOD'S PEOPLE

IN THE WORD

THE GIFT OF EXHORTATION

You've probably been around people who have a real gift for encouraging others. They have the unique ability to make you feel special. Their ministry of comfort, challenge and counsel helps and heals discouraged people.

The word exhortation means "to come alongside." Exhorting someone is coming alongside that person for the sake of encouraging and advising him or her.

Do you know someone who has the gift of exhortation? Who?

_____

_____

What are the qualities or characteristics that help you to see that he or she has this special gift?

_____

_____

The apostle Paul had the gift of exhortation. As you read the Book of Acts you will see that Paul was an encouragement to others even after enduring brutal beatings, mobs and imprisonment.

How did Paul use his gift of exhortation in these Scripture passages?

Acts 14:21,22 _____

Acts 20:17-35 _____

Another New Testament Christian who stands out as possessing the gift of exhortation is Barnabas. In fact, everywhere Barnabas appears in the Bible he is encouraging someone.

According to Acts 4:36, what does the name Barnabas mean?

_____

_____

Read Acts 11:19-26. List several ways Barnabas was an encouragement to the believers in Antioch.

_____

_____

How was Barnabas an encouragement to Paul in Acts 9:27?

_____

_____

You might need to read the entire account of Paul's conversion in chapter 9 for a clearer understanding. Barnabas and Paul left the church in Antioch and began to preach around the world (Acts 13). On their first long trip Barnabas wanted to take his nephew John (called Mark) who Barnabas saw as a potential Christian leader. (Barnabas saw and encouraged potential in people.) John Mark didn't make it through the entire trip and left to return to Jerusalem (Acts 13:13). After the first trip was completed, Paul and Barnabas decided to go back to visit the places they had

IN THE WORD

ENCOURAGING
GOD'S PEOPLE

been (see Acts 15:36). Again Barnabas wanted to take John Mark, but Paul insisted they shouldn't take him since he deserted them earlier. A sharp disagreement broke out. Paul thought of the work; Barnabas thought of the man (see Acts 15:37-41).

Read Acts 15:36-41. What was the result of the argument (see vv. 39,40.)?

If you were Paul, would you have given John Mark a second chance? Why or why not?

What characteristics made Barnabas a good friend?

We might be missing half of the New Testament books had Barnabas not used his gift of encouragement. Although Barnabas never wrote a book in the New Testament, Paul wrote 13 and Mark wrote one—and Barnabas encouraged them both!

So What?

Who in your life needs your encouragement?

What specifically will you do to encourage them?

Encouragement One

Encouragement Two

Encouragement Three

THINGS TO THINK ABOUT

1. Why is it sometimes difficult to encourage others?

....

....

....

2. The gift of exhortation involves encouragement and sometimes confrontation. Why is it difficult to confront some-one even though you know it will help him or her get back on the right path?

....

....

....

3. The word exhortation means "to come alongside." After all that you have learned about encouragement, what do you think this will come to mean in your own life?

....

....

....

ENCOURAGING GOD'S PEOPLE

 **PARENT PAGE**

AFFIRMATION BOMBARDMENT

"Let us not give up meeting together, as some are in the habit of doing, but let us encourage one another—and all the more as you see the Day approaching" (Hebrews 10:25).

What does this verse say about encouragement?

_____

_____

_____

In what ways do you need to be encouraged today?

_____

_____

Bring together your entire family. Now take each family member one at a time and bombard them with affirming and encouraging words. Start with one family member and have everyone else offer them at least one affirming comment. Before you move to the next family member, pray for this person.

Session 5 "Encouraging God's People"
Date _____

GIVING IT AWAY

KEY VERSES

"We have different gifts, according to the grace given us. If a man's gift is prophesying, let him use it in proportion to his faith. If it is serving, let him serve; if it is teaching, let him teach; if it is encouraging, let him encourage; if it is contributing to the needs of others, let him give generously; if it is leadership, let him govern diligently; if it is showing mercy, let him do it cheerfully."
Romans 12:6-8

BIBLICAL BASIS

Matthew 6:3,4;
Mark 12:41-44;
Luke 12:48;
Acts 20:35;
2 Corinthians 8:1-7; 9:6-8;
Romans 12:6-8;
1 Timothy 6:10,17-19

THE BIG IDEA

A person with the gift of giving takes the focus off his or her personal "wealth" and places the focus on giving freely and cheerfully to the Body of Christ.

AIMS OF THIS SESSION

During this session you will guide students to:
• Examine the spiritual gift of giving;
• Discover the possibility of using this God-given gift;
• Implement a decision to develop an attitude of giving from a Christian perspective.

CHECK IT OUT

THE GIFT OF GIVING—
Students rate their aptitudes in the gift of giving.

TEAM EFFORT— JUNIOR HIGH/ MIDDLE SCHOOL

GIVING HANDS—
Discussing thoughts on giving.

TEAM EFFORT— HIGH SCHOOL

THE GIVING GAME—
Students try to give away money.

IN THE WORD

THE GIFT OF GIVING—
A Bible study exploring the various aspects of giving.

THINGS TO THINK ABOUT (OPTIONAL)

Questions to get students thinking and talking about their attitudes concerning money.

PARENT PAGE

A tool to get the session into the home and allow parents and young people to discuss giving.

LEADER'S DEVOTIONAL

"But just as you excel in everything—in faith, in speech, in knowledge, in complete earnestness and in your love for us—see that you also excel in this grace of giving" (2 Corinthians 8:7).

When I was in high school, no one ever taught me the importance of giving. Not being eager to part with what little cash I had, I never knew what a great privilege giving was. My youth pastor never talked about it. I never heard very many sermons in church about it. All I knew was that when the basket was passed, I was "supposed" to throw in a couple bucks.

As an adult, I have been fortunate to learn how to grow in the grace of giving. I've also seen this principle at work in other people's lives. There was a father of a couple guys in our youth ministry who didn't even attend our church. Every so often I'd receive a phone call from him and he'd ask me, "What kinds of needs do you have in your youth ministry?" We'd talk for awhile and then, a few days later, I'd receive a check in the mail to invest in the lives of young people. This dad knew how to excel in the grace of giving. He blessed countless lives by giving to others what God had given to him.

Giving is a wonderful way to free yourself from the trappings of materialism and the desire to hoard riches. Giving, not only monetarily but also of your time and talents, is one of the most practical, spiritual investments you could ever make. When you teach young people to be cheerful, generous givers, you are equipping them to understand how to be a good steward of all God has given them. You also help them to receive the wonderful blessings God pours out to those who trust Him with everything. (Written by Joey O'Connor.)

"We don't suddenly, someday, have an abundance of time and money to give. We begin with the little pieces. We are in training now, learning bit by bit to manage money, power, time, relationships and temptation. Then maybe someday we will find ourselves competent to manage life on a grander scale."
—Lynn Anderson

GIVING IT AWAY

K EY VERSES

"We have different gifts, according to the grace given us. If a man's gift is prophesying, let him use it in proportion to his faith. If it is serving, let him serve; if it is teaching, let him teach; if it is encouraging, let him encourage; if it is contributing to the needs of others, let him give generously; if it is leadership, let him govern diligently; if it is showing mercy, let him do it cheerfully." Romans 12:6-8

B IBLICAL BASIS

Matthew 6:3,4; Mark 12:41-44; Luke 12:48; Acts 20:35; 2 Corinthians 8:1-7; 9:6-8; Romans 12:6-8; 1 Timothy 6:10,17-19

T HE BIG IDEA

A person with the gift of giving takes the focus off his or her personal "wealth" and places the focus on giving freely and cheerfully to the body of Christ.

C HECK IT OUT (5-10 MINUTES)

THE GIFT OF GIVING

• Give each student a copy of "The Gift of Giving" on page 99 and a pen or pencil.
• Have students complete the page.
On a scale of 1-10 rate your responses to these statements:

1	2	3	4	5	6	7	8	9	10
NO		rarely		maybe		sometimes			YES!

_____ I see myself as a person who is very generous when it comes to giving money to my church.
_____ I enjoy giving money to the needy.
_____ I have a strong desire to use my money wisely, knowing God will direct my giving.
_____ I am confident that God will take care of my needs when I give sacrificially and cheerfully.
_____ I believe I have the gift of giving.

Why was this important to Jesus?

Attitude Check Four: Give what you have.
Read Luke 12:48. What does Jesus mean when He says, "From everyone who has been given much, much will be demanded"?

SO WHAT?
How does this study relate to your life?

What decisions (if any) do you want to make about giving?

T HINGS TO THINK ABOUT (OPTIONAL)

• Use the questions on page 103 after or as a part of "In the Word."
1. How can money affect the way we view life?

2. Do you think God gives mainly to rich people the gift of giving?

3. Compared to the world's standards, what is rich?

P ARENT PAGE

• Distribute page to parents.

Team Effort—Junior High/Middle School (15-20 Minutes)

Giving Hands

- Display a copy of "Giving Hands" on page 101 using an overhead projector.
- Read the following poem with the students.
- Discuss the questions.
- Read the following poem about giving.

One by one He took them from me
All the things I valued most;
'Til I was empty-handed,
Every glittering toy was lost.

And I walked earth's highways, grieving,
In my rags and poverty.
Until I heard His voice inviting,
"Lift those empty hands to Me!"

Then I turned my hands toward heaven,
And He filled them with a store
Of His own transcendent riches,
'Til they could contain no more.

And at last I comprehended
with my stupid mind, and dull
That God cannot pour His riches
Into hands already full.

—Source Unknown

How does this poem relate to the gift of giving?

What is your family's policy on giving?

Team Effort—High School (15-20 Minutes)

The Giving Game

- Make sure everyone in your group has change (dimes, nickels, pennies) in their hands and have them stand up. Then tell them they have a short amount of time to *give away* as much money to one another as they possibly can. (They will have fun, lots of laughter and movement).
- Then have them stop. When they all look toward you tell them "Now get as much money as you possibly can." At first they will laugh, but eventually the majority will just stand still and stop playing the game. Have them sit down.
- Share: In Acts 20:35 Jesus said, "It is more blessed to give than to receive."
- Discuss the following questions:

Fold

How did you feel when you were giving the money away?
Did you notice that the noise level was quieter during the "get" part of this experience? Why?
How does Acts 20:35 relate to this experience?
What principles do you see in this Scripture?

In The Word (25-30 Minutes)

The Gift of Giving

- Divide students into groups of three or four.
- Give each student a copy of "The Gift of Giving" on pages 103 and 105 and a pen or pencil.
- Have students complete the Bible study.
The gift of giving is the special ability that God gives to certain members of the Body of Christ to contribute their material resources to the work of the Lord with liberality and cheerfulness.
Read 2 Corinthians 8:1-7.

(v. 2) 1. Were the Macedonian people wealthy?

(v. 2) 2. What did they have in place of money?

(v. 3) 3. How much did they give?

(v. 4) 4. What was their attitude in giving?

(v. 5) 5. Why do you suppose they had such a good attitude about giving?

Paul explains the gift this way: "And since we have gifts that differ according to the grace given to us, let each exercise them accordingly...he who gives, with liberality" (Romans 12:6,8, *NASB*).
Another interpretation says: "If God has given you money, be generous..." (Romans 12:8, *TLB*).
Here are some principles to help you become a better giver:

Attitude Check One: Give without boasting.
Read Matthew 6:3,4. Why do you think we should give in secret?

Attitude Check Two: Give with a proper perspective.
Read 1 Timothy 6:10. This often-misquoted passage doesn't say "money is the root of all evil" but "the love of money is a root of all kinds of evil." What is the danger of loving money?

What unhealthy attitudes show up in people who live for money?

Attitude Check Three: Give sacrificially.
Read Mark 12:41-44. Why was the widow honored more than the rich people?

GIVING IT AWAY

HECK IT OUT

THE GIFT OF GIVING

On a scale of 1-10 rate your responses to these statements:

1	2	3	4	5	6	7	8	9	10
NO		rarely		maybe		sometimes		YES!	

.... I see myself as a person who is very generous when it comes to giving money to my church.

.... I enjoy giving money to the needy.

.... I have a strong desire to use my money wisely, knowing God will direct my giving.

.... I am confident that God will take care of my needs when I give sacrificially and cheerfully.

.... I believe I have the gift of giving.

 EAM EFFORT

GIVING HANDS

Read the following poem about giving.

> One by one He took them from me
>> All the things I valued most;
> 'Til I was empty-handed,
>> Every glittering toy was lost.
> And I walked earth's highways, grieving.
>> In my rags and poverty.
> Until I heard His voice inviting,
>> "Lift those empty hands to Me!"
> Then I turned my hands toward heaven,
>> And He filled them with a store
> Of His own transcendent riches,
>> 'Til they could contain no more.
> And at last I comprehended
>> with my stupid mind, and dull
> That God cannot pour His riches
>> Into hands already full.
>
>> —Source Unknown

How does this poem relate to the gift of giving?

What is your family's policy on giving?

IN THE WORD

GIVING IT AWAY

THE GIFT OF GIVING

The gift of giving is the special ability that God gives to certain members of the Body of Christ to contribute their material resources to the work of the Lord with liberality and cheerfulness. Read 2 Corinthians 8:1-7.

(v. 2) 1. Were the Macedonian people wealthy? ....

(v. 2) 2. What did they have in place of money? ....

(v. 3) 3. How much did they give? ....

(v. 4) 4. What was their attitude in giving? ....

(v. 5) 5. Why do you suppose they had such a good attitude about giving? ....

Paul explains the gift this way: "And since we have gifts that differ according to the grace given to us, let each exercise them accordingly...he who gives, with liberality" (Romans 12:6,8, *NASB*).

Another interpretation says: "If God has given you money, be generous..." (Romans 12:8, *TLB*). Here are some principles to help you become a better giver:

Attitude Check One: Give without boasting.

Read Matthew 6:3,4. Why do you think we should give in secret?

Attitude Check Two: Give with a proper perspective.

Read 1 Timothy 6:10. This often-misquoted passage doesn't say "money is the root of all evil" but "the love of money is a root of all kinds of evil." What is the danger of loving money?

What unhealthy attitudes show up in people who live for money?

Attitude Check Three: Give sacrificially.

Read Mark 12:41-44. Why was the widow honored more than the rich people?

IN THE WORD

GIVING IT AWAY

Why was this important to Jesus?

....

Attitude Check Four: Give what you have.

Read Luke 12:48. What does Jesus mean when He says, "From everyone who has been given much, much will be demanded"?

....

....

SO WHAT?

How does this study relate to your life?

....

....

What decisions (if any) do you want to make about giving?

....

....

....

THINGS TO THINK ABOUT

1. How can money affect the way we view life?

....

....

2. Do you think God gives mainly to rich people the gift of giving?

....

....

3. Compared to the world's standards, what is rich?

....

....

....

PARENT PAGE

GIVING IT AWAY

SOWING AND REAPING

Read 1 Timothy 6:17-19. What does God require of a rich person?

....

....

Are you rich? Think about this question as you read this poem.

> "I asked God for strength that I might achieve.
>> I was made weak that I might learn humbly to obey.
> I asked God for health that I might do greater things.
>> I was given infirmity that I might do better things.
> I asked for riches that I might be happy.
>> I was given poverty that I might be wise.
> I asked for power that I might have the praise of men.
>> I was given weakness that I might feel the need of God.
> I asked for all things that I might enjoy life.
>> I was given life that I might enjoy all things.
> I got nothing I asked for but everything I had hoped for...
>> Almost despite myself my unspoken prayers were answered.
> I am among all men most richly blessed."
>
> —An Unknown Confederate Soldier

God has a purpose in giving.

Read Acts 20:35. What is the meaning of this simple yet profound statement?

....

....

....

Why do you think God wants us to give?

....

....

"Remember this: Whoever sows sparingly will also reap sparingly, and whoever sows generously will also reap generously. Each man should give what he has decided in his heart to give, not reluctantly or under compulsion, for God loves a cheerful giver. And God is able to make all grace abound to you, so that in all things at all times, having all that you need, you will abound in every good work" (2 Corinthians 9:6-8).

What should the giver's attitude be?

....

....

....

....

How will the giver reap plenty?

....

....

....

....

What is God's promise to the giver?

....

....

....

....

Session 6 "Giving It Away"
Date ....

TAKING TIME TO CARE

KEY VERSES

"We have different gifts, according to the grace given us. If a man's gift is prophesying, let him use it in proportion to his faith. If it is serving, let him serve; if it is teaching, let him teach." Romans 12:6,7

"And in the church God has appointed first of all apostles, second prophets, third teachers, then workers of miracles, also those having gifts of healing, those able to help others, those with gifts of administration, and those speaking in different kinds of tongues." 1 Corinthians 12:28

BIBLICAL BASIS

Matthew 19:30;
John 13:1-20;
Romans 12:6,7; 16:3-6;
1 Corinthians 12:28;
Philippians 2:3-11;
1 Peter 5:2

THE BIG IDEA

No matter what our spiritual gifts may be, we are all called into the ministry of serving and helping others.

AIMS OF THIS SESSION

During this session you will guide students to:
• Examine the spiritual gifts of serving and helping;
• Discover the importance of servanthood and helping in the Body of Christ;
• Implement decisions to become more others-centered.

CHECK IT OUT

THE GIFT OF SERVING/ THE GIFT OF HELPING—

Students rate their aptitudes in the gifts of serving and helping.

TEAM EFFORT— JUNIOR HIGH/ MIDDLE SCHOOL

CHRIST THE SERVANT: CHECK HIS SERVE—

Students brainstorm a list of Christ's acts of service.

TEAM EFFORT— HIGH SCHOOL

SERVANT CHARADES—

A game to discover different types of service.

IN THE WORD

THE GIFT OF SERVING/THE GIFT OF HELPING—

A Bible study exploring the various aspects of serving and helping.

THINGS TO THINK ABOUT (OPTIONAL)

Questions to get students thinking and talking about the role of a servant.

PARENT PAGE

A tool to get the session into the home and allow parents and young people to discuss being a servant like Christ.

LEADER'S DEVOTIONAL

"Be shepherds of God's flock that is under your care, serving as overseers —not because you must, but because you are willing, as God wants you to be; not greedy for money, but eager to serve" (1 Peter 5:2).

Most youth workers know that youth ministry isn't the place to look for applause, standing ovations and visits to the Oval Office. Much of youth ministry happens through the secret, invisible work of volunteer youth workers who just may be someone like you. I have seen countless volunteers on our youth ministry team helping out teenagers in incredible ways that most people would never even think of. Like Mary who scrubs out pots of dry, crusted spaghetti on our camping trips after everyone has eaten. No applause, no attention drawn to her. Or Pete who faithfully woke up at 6:00 AM on Sunday mornings to mop a bandroom floor covered with sticky wrappers, spilled Coke and smelly, muddy grass so teenagers would have a clean place to sit during our Sunday morning program. Add that along with volunteers who have spent countless late-night hours counseling students, surviving ten-hour bus rides and sleeping in the dirt during Mexico mission trips. These people are my heroes. These people really care.

I'd venture to say that most youth workers, in one way or another, have the spiritual gifts of serving and helping. You can see it in the ways they meet the unique needs of teenagers. You can see it in their attitudes. And in their smiles. By using their gifts of serving and helping young people be all that God has designed them to be, youth workers model a selfless, others-centered way of living. That's living the life of Christ in full color. If you are serving and helping young people in the name of Jesus Christ, you can bet He's getting a standing ovation in heaven. That's what giving glory to God is all about. Keep up the good work. (Written by Joey O'Connor.)

"When Christ calls a man, He bids him come and die."—Dietrich Bonhoeffer

TAKING TIME TO CARE

KEY *VERSES*

"We have different gifts, according to the grace given us. If a man's gift is prophesying, let him use it in proportion to his faith. If it is serving, let him serve; if it is teaching, let him teach." Romans 12:6,7

"And in the church God has appointed first of all apostles, second prophets, third teachers, then workers of miracles, also those having gifts of healing, those able to help others, those with gifts of administration, and those speaking in different kinds of tongues." 1 Corinthians 12:28

BIBLICAL *BASIS*

Matthew 19:30; John 13:1-20; Romans 12:6,7; 16:3-6; 1 Corinthians 12:28; Philippians 2:3-11; 1 Peter 5:2

THE *BIG IDEA*

No matter what our spiritual gifts may be, we are all called into the ministry of serving and helping others.

CHECK *IT OUT* (5-10 MINUTES)

THE GIFT OF SERVING/THE GIFT OF HELPING

• Give each student a copy of "The Gift of Serving/The Gift of Helping" on page 113 and a pen or pencil.

• Have students complete the page.

THE GIFT OF SERVING

On a scale of 1-10 rate your responses to these statements:

1	2	3	4	5	6	7	8	9	10
NO		rarely		maybe		sometimes			YES!

____ I could be described as an "others-centered" person.

____ I enjoy meeting the needs of others.

____ You'll frequently find me volunteering my time to help with the needs of the church.

____ I'm the type of person that likes to reach out to less fortunate people.

Which of these attitudes and qualities would you like to have in your own life?

So WHAT?

What specific ways can you serve and help in each of the following areas?

Home _____ School _____ Church _____

THINGS TO *THINK ABOUT* (OPTIONAL)

• Use the questions on page 115 after or as a part of "In the Word."

1. What is it that you enjoy about the people you consider servants?

2. After looking at this session, what are some of the "thankless" jobs you now have a better appreciation for at church and home?

3. "The call to Christ is the call to serve." What does this phrase mean to you?

PARENT *PAGE*

• Distribute page to parents.

Fold

⫶ III ⫶

I feel good when I help with the routine jobs at the church.

I believe I have the gift of serving.

THE GIFT OF HELPING

On a scale of 1-10 rate your responses to these statements:

1	2	3	4	5	6	7	8	9	10
NO		rarely		maybe			sometimes		YES!

You'll often find me volunteering to do "behind the scenes" activities that few notice but must be done.

I'm the one who often cleans up after the meeting without being asked.

I seldom think twice before doing a task that might not bring me praise.

I receive joy doing jobs that others see as "thankless."

I am able to do jobs that others won't do, and I feel good about myself.

I believe I have the gift of helping.

TEAM EFFORT—JUNIOR HIGH/ MIDDLE SCHOOL (15-20 MINUTES)

CHRIST THE SERVANT: CHECK HIS SERVE

• Divide students into teams.

• Give each team a piece of paper and a pencil. The object of the game is for each team to come up with as many <u>unique</u> ways as they can that Jesus served people. To win, a team must come up with the most acts of service that are not listed by the other teams.

Give the students three minutes to list all the ways they can remember that Jesus served others. Have each team keep their own score. Starting with team one, have each team read their list. If, as they are reading, another team has that act on their list, then that act is crossed off both lists and neither team gets a point for that act. When all the lists are read, the team with the most acts of service remaining is the winner.

TEAM EFFORT—HIGH SCHOOL (15-20 MINUTES)

SERVANT CHARADES

• Divide students into groups of from 3 to 8 students.

• Give the groups only five minutes to create a short drama about a way they could serve someone else. Have them perform for the entire group and then have others guess the act of service.

IN THE WORD (25-30 MINUTES)

THE GIFT OF SERVING/THE GIFT OF HELPING

• Divide students into groups of three or four.

• Give each student a copy of "In the Word" on pages 115 and 117 and a pen or pencil, or

display a copy using an overhead projector.

• Have students complete the Bible study.

THE GIFT OF SERVING

The call to Christ is the call to serve! "We have different gifts, according to the grace given us... Let [each] use it in proportion to his faith. If it is serving, let him serve" (Romans 12:6,7).

What do you think would happen to the church if no one in the Body exercised the gift of serving?

Brainstorm together roles/tasks within the church that couldn't be done without servants.

Leonard Bernstein, the famous orchestra conductor, was asked, "What is the most difficult instrument to play?" He responded:

Second fiddle. I can get plenty of first violinists, but to find one who plays second violin with as much enthusiasm, or second French horn or second flute, now that's a problem. And yet if no one plays second, we have no harmony.

Read Matthew 19:30. How does this verse relate to the quote about being second fiddle?

What does Jesus mean when He says the "last shall be first?"

Read John 13:1-20. Why did Jesus wash the disciples' feet?

Do you think this attitude of servanthood was a part of the daily life of Jesus? Explain your answer.

THE GIFT OF HELPING

"And in the church God has appointed...those able to help others" (1 Corinthians 12:28).

The gift of helping is the special ability to assist others to increase their effectiveness in life. The person with the gift of helping is often a background person who makes things happen without being noticed. Even though this gift is often overlooked, it is a vital act of ministry in the Christian church.

Do you know people with the gift of helping? Who are they and what do they do?

In Paul's letters he often mentions faithful helpers. These helpers were apparently the backbone of the early church. These faithful helpers freed up Paul and the leaders to do mighty works of ministry. Without the helpers there would have been no Pauls and Peters in the early church.

Read Romans 16:3-6. What did Priscilla and Aquila do for the Lord?

What is mentioned about Mary in verse 6?

What attitudes or qualities do you feel that a person with the gift of helping needs to have?

TAKING
TIME TO CARE

HECK IT OUT

THE GIFT OF SERVING/THE GIFT OF HELPING

The Gift of Serving

On a scale of 1-10 rate your responses to these statements:

1	2	3	4	5	6	7	8	9	10
NO		rarely		maybe			sometimes		YES!

.... I could be described as an "others-centered" person.

.... I enjoy meeting the needs of others.

.... You'll frequently find me volunteering my time to help with the needs of the church.

.... I'm the type of person that likes to reach out to less fortunate people.

.... I feel good when I help with the routine jobs at the church.

.... I believe I have the gift of serving.

The Gift of Helping

On a scale of 1-10 rate your responses to these statements:

1	2	3	4	5	6	7	8	9	10
NO		rarely		maybe			sometimes		YES!

.... You'll often find me volunteering to do "behind the scenes" activities that few notice but must be done.

.... I'm the one who often cleans up after the meeting without being asked.

.... I seldom think twice before doing a task that might not bring me praise.

.... I receive joy doing jobs that others see as "thankless."

.... I am able to do jobs that others won't do, and I feel good about myself.

.... I believe I have the gift of helping.

IN THE WORD

THE GIFT OF SERVING/THE GIFT OF HELPING

The Gift of Serving

"The call to Christ is the call to serve!" Perhaps you have the gift of serving! "We have different gifts, according to the grace given us... Let [each] use it in proportion to his faith. If it is serving, let him serve..." (Romans 12:6,7).

What do you think would happen to the church if no one in the Body exercised the gift of serving?

Brainstorm together roles/tasks within the church that couldn't be done without servants.

Leonard Bernstein, the famous orchestra conductor, was asked, "What is the most difficult instrument to play?" He responded:

> Second fiddle. I can get plenty of first violinists, but to find one who plays second violin with as much enthusiasm, or second French horn or second flute, now that's a problem. And yet if no one plays second, we have no harmony.

Read Matthew 19:30. How does this verse relate to the quote about being second fiddle?

What does Jesus mean when He says the "last shall be first?"

Read John 13:1-20. Why did Jesus wash the disciples' feet?

Do you think this attitude of servanthood was a part of the daily life of Jesus? Explain your answer.

Do you know people with the gift of helping? Who are they and what do they do?

The Gift of Helping

"And in the church God has appointed...those able to help others" (1 Corinthians 12:28).

The gift of helping is the special ability to assist others to increase their effectiveness in life. The person with the gift of helping is often a background person who makes things happen without being noticed. Even though this gift is often overlooked, it is a vital act of ministry in the Christian church.

TAKING
TIME TO CARE

IN THE WORD

In Paul's letters he often mentions faithful helpers. These helpers were apparently the backbone of the early church. These faithful helpers freed up Paul and the leaders to do mighty works of ministry. Without the helpers there would have been no Pauls and Peters in the early church.

Read Romans 16:3-6. What did Priscilla and Aquila do for the Lord?

What is mentioned about Mary in verse 6?

What attitudes or qualities do you feel that a person with the gift of helping needs to have?

Which of these attitudes and qualities would you like to have in your own life?

SO WHAT?

What specific ways can you serve and help in each of the following areas?

Home   School   Church

THINGS TO THINK ABOUT

1. What is it that you enjoy about the people you consider servants?

2. After looking at this session, what are some of the "thankless" jobs you now have a better appreciation for at church and home?

3. "The call to Christ is the call to serve." What does this phrase mean to you?

PARENT PAGE

PUTTING OTHERS BEFORE YOURSELF

Read Philippians 2:3-11. How does Paul suggest we live our lives according to verses 3 and 4?

....

....

....

What is the central theme of verses 5 through 8?

....

....

....

What is the result of Christ's obedience and service according to verses 9 though 11?

....

....

....

What specific areas of your life need changing so that you can be more of a servant?

....

....

....

How could this concept help our family?

....

....

....

Session 7 "Taking Time to Care"

Date ....

THE OPEN HEART

K EY VERSES

"If it is encouraging, let him encourage; if it is contributing to the needs of others, let him give generously; if it is leadership, let him govern diligently; if it is show-ing mercy, let him do it cheerfully. Share with God's people who are in need. Practice hospitality." Romans 12:8,13

B IBLICAL BASIS

Matthew 5:7,16; 10:42; 25:31-46;
Luke 10:30-37;
Acts 9:43; 16:15,33,34;
Romans 12:6,8,13;
1 Peter 4:9;
Revelation 3:20

T HE BIG IDEA

The gifts of mercy and hospitality manifest themselves in individuals who are others-centered. These people focus on being sensitive to those who have needs.

A IMS OF THIS SESSION

During this session you will guide students to:
- Examine the spiritual gifts of mercy and hospitality;
- Discover the importance and necessity of service-oriented lifestyles;
- Implement a decision to practical-ly care for the poor and oppressed.

C HECK IT OUT

THE GIFT OF MERCY/THE GIFT OF HOSPITALITY—
Students rate their aptitudes in the gifts of mercy and hospitality.

T EAM EFFORT— JUNIOR HIGH/ MIDDLE SCHOOL

SERVING THE POOR IS SERVING JESUS—
A story illustrating mercy.

T EAM EFFORT— HIGH SCHOOL

SHOWING MERCY—
Students are challenged to think of practical ways to help those in need.

I N THE WORD

THE GIFT OF MERCY/THE GIFT OF HOSPITALITY—
A Bible study on the various aspects of mercy and hospitality.

T HINGS TO THINK ABOUT (OPTIONAL)

Questions to get students thinking and talking about showing mercy and hospitality to others.

P ARENT PAGE

A tool to get the session into the home and allow parents and young people to discuss how the family can show compassion to others.

LEADER'S DEVOTIONAL

"Here I am! I stand at the door and knock. If anyone hears my voice and opens the door, I will come in and eat with him, and he with me" (Revelation 3:20).

Some of my fondest youth ministry memories are the times when Krista and I had young people over for a meal. Breakfast, lunch, dinner, late night snacks—we've sat around our table with students at all hours of the day and night. In fact, just last night we had about fifteen college-age people over to our home for a barbecue. We've known some of these people since they were freshmen in high school and now they're all getting married! It is a wonderful privilege to see God's continued work in their lives. In fact, some of these "former" students are becoming very special friends.

As we grow in our relationship with Jesus, I believe He wants us to become closer and closer friends with Him. He wants to take us to new depths in our understanding of who He is and how we can know Him better. Every day, He wants us to invite Him into our homes. Jesus wants to sit down and chat. He wants to share a meal with us. The message of Revelation 3:20 is that we have the opportunity to show hospitality to Jesus every day.

How can you keep Jesus locked out of your heart? By being too busy! Your schedule as a youth worker can be very demanding, but you will never be able to compare the deep joy and satisfaction that comes from meeting with God every day. As you study the spiritual gifts of mercy and hospitality, my hope is that you are refreshed by the mercy of God and in response, you renew your desire to meet with Jesus today. He is knocking on the door of your heart, waiting for you to invite him in. Before opening your door to students, open your heart to Jesus first. (Written by Joey O'Connor.)

"It's only by His mercy that we are not destroyed totally and completely. Therefore, we should be imitators of God and show mercy to those God brings our way."—Elliot Johnson/ Al Schierbaum

THE OPEN HEART

KEY VERSES

"If it is encouraging, let him encourage; if it is contributing to the needs of others, let him give generously; if it is leadership, let him govern diligently; if it is showing mercy, let him do it cheerfully. Share with God's people who are in need. Practice hospitality." Romans 12:8,13

BIBLICAL BASIS

Matthew 5:7,16; 10:42; 25:31-46; Luke 10:30-37; Acts 9:43; 16:15,33,34; Romans 12:6,8,13; 1 Peter 4:9; Revelation 3:20

THE BIG IDEA

The gifts of mercy and hospitality manifest themselves in individuals who are others-centered. These people focus on being sensitive to those who have needs.

CHECK IT OUT (5-10 MINUTES)

THE GIFT OF MERCY/THE GIFT OF HOSPITALITY

• Give each student a copy of "The Gift of Mercy/The Gift of Hospitality" on page 125 and a pen or pencil.

• Have students complete the page.

THE GIFT OF MERCY

On a scale of 1-10 rate your responses to these statements:

1	2	3	4	5	6	7	8	9	10
NO		rarely		maybe			sometimes		YES!

_____ I enjoy giving hope to those in need (such as the lonely, elderly or shut-ins).

_____ I would like to have a ministry with those who are needy.

_____ I would like to visit rest homes and other institutions where people need visitors.

_____ I am very compassionate to those in need.

_____ I have a desire to work with people who have special physical needs.

_____ I believe I have the gift of mercy.

Read 1 Peter 4:9. Why do you think Paul adds "ungrudgingly" (*RSV*) or "without grumbling" (*NIV*) when he speaks of being hospitable?

So What?

Will you commit yourself to acting with mercy in one of the areas of need you have listed above? Which one?

What will you do?

If you know someone with the gift of hospitality, why not write them a short note today expressing your gratitude for their generosity?

THINGS TO THINK ABOUT (OPTIONAL)

• Use the questions on page 129 after or as a part of "In the Word."

1. Who are people you know who have the gift of mercy or hospitality?

   What special traits do you see in their lives?

2. Even if someone didn't have the gift of mercy as a spiritual gift, do you think it would be a necessary attitude for a Christian to strive after? Why or why not?

3. Are there a variety of ways in which the gift of hospitality can be used? If so, what are some of those ways?

PARENT PAGE

• Distribute page to parents.

THE GIFT OF HOSPITALITY

On a scale of 1-10 rate your responses to these statements:

1	2	3	4	5	6	7	8	9	10
NO		rarely		maybe		sometimes			YES!

_____ When people are in need I enjoy having them in my home. I do not feel like they are intruding.

_____ I enjoy having strangers in my home.

_____ I like making strangers feel comfortable.

_____ I believe God has given me the ability to make others feel comfortable in my home.

_____ I want my house to always be a spot where people in need can come and find rest.

_____ I believe I have the gift of hospitality.

TEAM EFFORT—JUNIOR HIGH/MIDDLE SCHOOL (15-20 MINUTES)

SERVING THE POOR IS SERVING JESUS

• Divide the students into groups of three or four.

• Give each student a copy of "Serving the Poor Is Serving Jesus" on page 127 and a pen or pencil, or display a copy using an overhead projector.

• Have the students complete their papers in the small groups.

What do you think about the phrase "when we serve the poor, we serve Jesus"?

Read Matthew 25:31-46. What were the specific actions Jesus mentioned in this passage of scripture?

What was the attitude of the people in verses 37-39? verse 44?

What point is Jesus making in verse 40?

TEAM EFFORT—HIGH SCHOOL (15-20 MINUTES)

SHOWING MERCY

• Read the following paragraph to the whole group, then discuss the questions at the end.

Jake has stood at the corner near your school every day for at least a year. He is homeless, a little crazy, very poor and often drunk. All of the students make fun of him. He definitely is an easy target for ridicule. One evening at youth group your youth worker challenges your whole group to "serve the poor and oppressed." He says there are more verses in the Bible about caring for the poor than verses on salvation. All he asks is that you pray and ask God to put a name of a needy person into your mind. You pray, and loud and clear the name that comes to your mind is Jake—accompanied by the scene you have seen a hundred times with him standing on the corner, begging for money.

What are several ways you can help Jake?

Are there any Scriptures that come to your mind when you think of this situation?

IN THE WORD (25-30 MINUTES)

THE GIFT OF MERCY/THE GIFT OF HOSPITALITY

• Divide students into groups of three or four.

• Give each student a copy of "In the Word" on pages 129 and 131 and a pen or pencil.

• Have students complete the Bible study.

THE GIFT OF MERCY

The gift of mercy is a gift that gets little recognition yet has great personal rewards. "And since we have gifts that differ according to the grace given to us, let each exercise them accordingly...he who shows mercy, with cheerfulness" (Romans 12:6,8, *NASB*).

To have mercy means to be kind or compassionate. It means to relieve suffering. *Webster's Dictionary* defines mercy as "the quality in something experienced or observed which arouses feelings of pity, sorrow, sympathy or compassion."

The gift of mercy may be demonstrated by direct personal involvement with the sick, outcast, poor, aged, mentally ill, deformed, hungry, shut-in, retarded, deprived, widowed, sad, underprivileged, alcoholic or handicapped. A person with the gift of mercy wants intensely to meet the needs of those who hurt.

Read Luke 10:30-37. What specific acts of mercy did the Samaritan perform?

This man not only felt sorry—he *acted!*

In the book of Acts a jailer became a Christian in the presence of Paul and Silas. What acts of mercy did this jailer do to help Paul and Silas? (See Acts 16:33,34.)

What do you think are the areas of greatest need in your community?

In the world?

What achievable steps could you take to show mercy in these areas?

THE GIFT OF HOSPITALITY

If you enjoy organizing and hosting a party, making strangers feel welcome or sharing with those in need, you may have the gift of hospitality. "Practice hospitality" (Romans 12:13, *RSV*), "Practice hospitality ungrudgingly to one another" (1 Peter 4:9, *RSV*).

Look up the verses below and list the name of the person who was hospitable and what he or she did.

Name	Act of Hospitality
Acts 9:43	
Acts 16:15	
Acts 16:34	

In the days of Jesus and in the days of the early church, people were dependent on others for food and lodging as they traveled from city to city. Do you think there is still a need for the gift of hospitality today with all the restaurants, motels and hotels that are available to travelers? Explain your thoughts.

Whether you have the gift of hospitality or not, what can you do to develop a stronger attitude of hospitality?

THE OPEN HEART

 **C**HECK IT OUT

THE GIFT OF MERCY/THE GIFT OF HOSPITALITY

The Gift of Mercy
On a scale of 1-10 rate your responses to these statements:

1	2	3	4	5	6	7	8	9	10
NO		rarely		maybe		sometimes			YES!

_____ I enjoy giving hope to those in need (such as the lonely, elderly or shut-ins).

_____ I would like to have a ministry with those who are needy.

_____ I would like to visit rest homes and other institutions where people need visitors.

_____ I am very compassionate to those in need.

_____ I have a desire to work with people who have special physical needs.

_____ I believe I have the gift of mercy.

The Gift of Hospitality
On a scale of 1-10 rate your responses to these statements:

1	2	3	4	5	6	7	8	9	10
NO		rarely		maybe		sometimes		YES!	

_____ When people are in need I enjoy having them in my home. I do not feel like they are intruding.

_____ I enjoy having strangers in my home.

_____ I like making strangers feel comfortable.

_____ I believe God has given me the ability to make others feel comfortable in my home.

_____ I want my house to always be a spot where people in need can come and find rest.

_____ I believe I have the gift of hospitality.

THE OPEN HEART

TEAM EFFORT

SERVING THE POOR IS SERVING JESUS

"'Whatever you did for one of the least of these brothers of mine, you did for me'" (Matthew 25:40). The Queshawa Indians in the mountains of Ecuador are an exceptionally beautiful people. They have high cheek bones, and other distinct features. They wear colorful beads. And they are extremely poor. Through Compassion International, my friend, Duffy Robbins, and his family sponsor a little boy named Javier in the little village of Octovolo, Ecuador. The Robbins family's $24 a month and periodic letters have given Javier health, Christianity and education.

Recently we had the opportunity to meet Javier and his family. One of the biggest events of his life was to meet Duffy, his sponsor. When we arrived in Octovolo, fifty kids were waiting for us. They ran up and touched us. Both Duffy and I are bald-headed and they loved patting the tops of our heads.

Then, as if on cue, the kids quieted down and Javier's family came through the middle of this group. Mom was carrying a baby, Dad was in his finest clothes (although he was without shoes), Grandma, Grandpa, aunts, uncles and I don't know how many brothers and sisters—all gathered around us. They invited us to to their home. Duffy and I were the only people wearing shoes as we walked up the mountain to Javier's home.

Their home was made of mud. They cooked in the corner of their one-room hut when it was cold, and there was no ventilation. These people were pitifully poor. No one wore shoes, no one had clean teeth and, from the looks of what they called a home, there was absolutely no furniture. The only picture on the wall was a photo of Duffy's family.

It was stuffy in the room and I thought I might get sick, so I excused myself. I walked outside thinking about all this poverty. I started to feel angry and a little hopeless. I sat down on a rock, looked toward the heavens and asked God, *Where is Jesus in the midst of their poverty?* And as clear as if it were yesterday I heard a strong, clear voice say, "Jesus is on the face of Javier." When we serve the poor, we serve Jesus.

What do you think about the phrase "when we serve the poor, we serve Jesus"?

Read Matthew 25:31-46. What were the specific actions Jesus mentioned in this passage of Scripture?

What was the attitude of the people in verses 37-39? verse 44?

What point is Jesus making in verse 40?

THE OPEN HEART

 N THE WORD

THE GIFT OF MERCY/THE GIFT OF HOSPITALITY

The Gift of Mercy

The gift of mercy is a gift that gets little recognition yet has great personal rewards. "And since we have gifts that differ according to the grace given to us, let each exercise them accordingly...he who shows mercy, with cheerfulness" (Romans 12:6,8, *NASB*).

To have mercy means to be kind or compassionate. It means to relieve suffering. *Webster's Dictionary* defines mercy as "the quality in something experienced or observed which arouses feelings of pity, sorrow, sympathy or compassion."

The gift of mercy may be demonstrated by direct personal involvement with the sick, outcast, poor, aged, mentally ill, deformed, hungry, shut-in, retarded, deprived, widowed, sad, underprivileged, alcoholic or handicapped. A person with the gift of mercy wants intensely to meet the needs of those who hurt.

Read Luke 10:30-37. What specific acts of mercy did the Samaritan perform?

....

....

This man not only felt sorry—he *acted*!

In the book of Acts, a jailer became a Christian in the presence of Paul and Silas. What acts of mercy did this jailer do to help Paul and Silas? (See Acts 16:33,34.)

....

....

What do you think are the areas of greatest need in your community?

....

....

In the world?

....

....

What achievable steps could you take to show mercy in these areas?

....

....

IN THE WORD

THE OPEN HEART

The Gift of Hospitality

If you enjoy organizing and hosting a party, making strangers feel welcome or sharing with those in need, you may have the gift of hospitality. "Practice hospitality" (Romans 12:13, *RSV*). "Practice hospitality ungrudgingly to one another" (1 Peter 4:9, *RSV*).

Look up the verses below and list the name of the person who was hospitable and what he or she did.

	Name	Act of Hospitality
Acts 9:43		
Acts 16:15		
Acts 16:34		

In the days of Jesus and in the days of the early church, people were dependent on others for food and lodging as they traveled from city to city. Do you think there is still a need for the gift of hospitality today with all the restaurants, motels and hotels that are available to travelers? Explain your thoughts.

Whether you have the gift of hospitality or not, what can you do to develop a stronger attitude of hospitality?

Read 1 Peter 4:9. Why do you think Paul adds "ungrudgingly" (*RSV*) or "without grumbling" (*NIV*) when he speaks of being hospitable?

So What?

Will you commit yourself to acting with mercy toward one of these needs? Which one?

What will you do?

If you know someone with the gift of hospitality, why not write them a short note today expressing your gratitude for their generosity?

THINGS TO THINK ABOUT

1. Who are people you know who have the gift of mercy or hospitality?

What special traits do you see in their lives?

2. Even if someone didn't have the gift of mercy as a spiritual gift, do you think it would be a necessary attitude for a Christian to strive for? Why or why not?

3. Are there a variety of ways in which the gift of hospitality can be used? If so, what are some of those ways?

PARENT PAGE

THE OPEN HEART

RAISING A COMPASSIONATE FAMILY

Look at the words of Jesus in the book of Matthew. What does each of the following verses say about showing mercy?

Meaning

Matthew 5:7 ....

Matthew 5:16 ....

Matthew 10:42 ....

Matthew 25:40 ....

Ideas for Showing Compassion

❑ Your family can save a child from hunger and malnutrition and give him or her a Christian education. Sponsor a Compassion child for $24 a month.

> Compassion International
> P.O. Box 7000
> Colorado Springs, CO 80933
> 800/336-7676

❑ Visit a rest home or convalescent hospital.
❑ Volunteer at a soup kitchen or thrift store.
❑ Invite a new family in your community over for dinner.
❑ Adopt a lonely single person.
❑ Call your pastor and ask how your family can serve others in need.
❑ Open up your home to an unwed mother.
❑ Become a financial sponsor of a youth organization like NIYM:

> National Institute of Youth Ministry
> 940 Calle Amanecer, Suite G
> San Clemente, CA 92673
> (714) 498-4418

The NIYM currently has ministries in:
❑ Ecuador,
❑ Urban youth ministry,
❑ Poland,
❑ Guatemala,
❑ youth ministry outreach.
❑ Bring a meal to a homeless person.
❑ Other ideas:

Who in our family needs our compassion? What will we do?

....
....
....

Who in our church family needs compassion? What will we do?

....
....
....

Who in our community needs compassion? What will we do?

....
....
....

Session 8 "The Open Heart"
Date ....

Unit III

SPIRITUAL GIFTS THAT PROVIDE COMMUNICATION AND LEADERSHIP

LEADER'S PEP TALK

When Doug was in 10th grade, I asked him to prepare a brief sermonette for a Youth Sunday program at our church. I love Youth Sundays, but as you know, the messages are usually strong with the heart and weak with the presentation. Doug stood before our congregation wearing a tie. He said, "Jim Burns and my parents asked me to dress up for my first sermon. I'm wearing a tie. Now that they have seen it on me...." He then took off his clip-on tie, placed it on the pulpit and gave the best Youth Sunday message I have heard to this day. Our pastor leaned over to me and said, "I think that young man is after my job!" From that day on I knew Doug had the spiritual gift of pastor/teacher. My job as his youth worker was to affirm his giftedness and give him lots of opportunity to use his gifts.

You have students in your group with pastoral abilities and other communication gifts. Your job is to help them understand they have those gifts and then give them every opportunity to use those gifts to the glory of God.

SHARING THE GOOD NEWS

K EY VERSES

"It was he who gave some to be apostles, some to be prophets, some to be evangelists, and some to be pastors and teachers."
Ephesians 4:11

"But everyone who prophesies speaks to men for their strengthening, encouragement and comfort."
1 Corinthians 14:3

B IBLICAL BASIS

Isaiah 52:7;
Matthew 28:16-20;
Acts 1:8; 8:12,35; 13:1-5;
15:32; 21:8;
1 Corinthians 14:1-5,39;
Ephesians 4:11;
2 Timothy 4:5

T HE BIG IDEA

The gifts of evangelism and prophecy communicate truth. The first is truth about God and the second is truth from God.

A IMS OF THIS SESSION

During this session you will guide students to:

- Examine the spiritual gifts of evangelism and prophecy;
- Discover the biblical principals behind these important gifts;
- Implement plans to share their faith.

C HECK IT OUT

THE GIFT OF EVANGELISM/THE GIFT OF PROPHECY—

Students rate their aptitudes in the gifts of evangelism and prophecy.

T EAM EFFORT— JUNIOR HIGH/ MIDDLE SCHOOL

CREATE AN OUTREACH EVENT—

Students plan how to reach out to their communities.

T EAM EFFORT— HIGH SCHOOL

THE LIFESAVING STATION—

A story and discussion to illustrate the importance of outreach in the church.

I N THE WORD

THE GIFT OF EVANGELISM/THE GIFT OF PROPHECY—

A Bible study exploring the various aspects of evangelism and prophecy.

T HINGS TO THINK ABOUT (OPTIONAL)

Questions to get students thinking and talking about applying evangelism and prophecy to their lives.

P ARENT PAGE

A tool to get the session into the home and allow parents and young people to discuss how their families can carry out the great commission.

LEADER'S DEVOTIONAL

"How beautiful on the mountains are the feet of those who bring good news, who proclaim peace, who bring good tidings, who proclaim salvation, who say to Zion, 'Your God reigns!'" (Isaiah 52:7).

Tom is a friend of mine who is one of the most contagious Christians I've ever known. In high school, Tom was heavily involved in the party scene and only came to our youth ministry a few times. During college, Tom finally became a Christian and his enthusiasm for Jesus hasn't died down yet. Whether at home, work, school or on the volleyball court, Tom is always looking for new ways to share the good news of Jesus Christ. Tom is a perfect example of what being an evangelist is all about.

One of the greatest myths in Christendom today is that you have to be the next Billy Graham in order to tell someone about Jesus. The devil would love to discourage all believers by having us compare ourselves to Billy Graham or someone like Tom. A lot of young people, including many youth workers, are flat out scared about sharing their faith. They're not very good evangelists and they know it.

If you or someone you know feels like this, it's important to remember that God doesn't keep a scorecard. He wants to free you of your fears of telling people about Him. And most of all, He doesn't want you to spend endless amounts of wasted time comparing yourself to others. Hopefully, this lesson will help you to look at evangelism and prophesy in a new light. You may not be a great evangelist but then again, the body of Christ isn't just a mouth, is it? (Written by Joey O'Connor.)

"The gospel is not theology. It's a Person. Theology doesn't save. Jesus Christ saves. The first-century disciples were totally involved with a Person. They were followers of Jesus. They were learners of Jesus. They were committed to Jesus. They were filled with Jesus."—Richard Halverson

Tear along perforation. Fold and place this Bible *Tuck-In*™ in your Bible for session use.

S E S S I O N N I N E B I B L E T U C K - I N ™

SHARING THE GOOD NEWS

— Fold —

 EY VERSES

"It was he who gave some to be apostles, some to be prophets, some to be evangelists, and some to be pastors and teachers." Ephesians 4:11

"But everyone who prophesies speaks to men for their strengthening, encouragement and comfort." 1 Corinthians 14:3

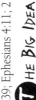 IBLICAL BASIS

Isaiah 52:7; Matthew 28:16-20; Acts 1:8; 8:12,35; 13:1-5; 15:32; 21:8; 1 Corinthians 14:1-5,39; Ephesians 4:11; 2 Timothy 4:5

T HE BIG IDEA

The gifts of evangelism and prophecy communicate truth. The first is truth about God and the second is truth from God.

C HECK IT OUT (5-10 MINUTES)

THE GIFT OF EVANGELISM/THE GIFT OF PROPHECY
• Give each student a copy of "The Gift of Evangelism/The Gift of Prophecy" on page 141 and a pen or pencil.
• Have students complete the page.

THE GIFT OF EVANGELISM
On a scale of 1-10 rate your responses to these statements:

1	2	3	4	5	6	7	8	9	10
NO		rarely		maybe			sometimes		YES!

_____ I can tell nonbelievers about my relationship with Christ in a comfortable manner.

_____ I always think of new ways in which I can share Christ with my non-Christian friends.

_____ I have the ability to direct conversations toward the message of Christ.

_____ I have led others to a personal relationship with Christ.

_____ I desire to learn more about God so I can share Him in a clearer way.

_____ I believe I have the gift of evangelism.

Acts 15:32

Read Acts 13:1-5. What were the responsibilities of Barnabas and Saul?

Paul stresses the importance of the gift of prophecy in 1 Corinthians 14:1-5,39. Read these verses. Why do you think Paul views prophecy as being so important?

What issues do you think a person with the gift of prophecy would speak on in the present day?

SO WHAT?
Do you know someone who has the gift of prophecy? If so, how does he or she make you feel when you hear him or her speak?

T HINGS TO THINK ABOUT (OPTIONAL)
• Use the questions on page 149 after or as a part of "In the Word."
1. What makes sharing our faith (evangelism) often a scary experience?

2. What makes the Christian faith attractive to nonbelievers?

What makes it *not* attractive?

3. Who is a modern-day prophet in your opinion and why?

P ARENT PAGE
• Distribute page to parents.

THE GIFT OF PROPHECY

On a scale of 1-10 rate your responses to these statements:

NO 1 2 3 4 5 6 7 8 9 10 YES!
    rarely   maybe   sometimes

___ I have given others important messages at the perfect time that I felt came from God.

___ I believe I have the ability to reveal God's truth about the future.

___ I desire to speak messages from God that will challenge people to change.

___ I have had the chance to proclaim God's truth at the required time.

___ I have given messages that were judgments from God.

___ I believe I have the gift of prophecy.

 ## TEAM EFFORT—JUNIOR HIGH/ MIDDLE SCHOOL (15-20 Minutes)

CREATE AN OUTREACH EVENT

It's a proven fact that people support what they create. Here's an opportunity to create an evangelistic outreach event which can make an eternal difference. Read Matthew 28:16-20. With the Great Commission in mind:

• List students' suggestions for several specific ways they can reach their communities for God.

• Now from those ideas help them create an outreach event. Make the plans, set a date, delegate responsibilities and pray for spiritual fruit.

 ## TEAM EFFORT—HIGH SCHOOL (25-30 Minutes)

THE LIFESAVING STATION

• Give each student a copy of "The Lifesaving Station" on page 143, or display a copy using an overhead projector.

• Read the story together and discuss the questions as a whole group.

1. When was the lifesaving station most effective?

2. Where did the lifesaving station go wrong?

3. How is the church like a lifesaving station?

What is the purpose of the church?

4. How can the church and this youth group do a better job of evangelism?

 # IN THE WORD (25-30 Minutes)

THE GIFT OF EVANGELISM/THE GIFT OF PROPHECY
THE GIFT OF EVANGELISM

• Divide students into groups of three or four.

• Give each student a copy of "In the Word" on pages 145 and 147 and a pen or pencil, or display a copy using an overhead projector.

• Have students complete the Bible study.

The word "evangelist" appears only three times in the entire New Testament (Acts 21:8, Ephesians 4:11, and 2 Timothy 4:5). In Ephesians 4:11 we read, "He gave some to be...evangelists." Though the word isn't used many times, its meaning is clearly defined. It means "one who proclaims the Good News."
Read Matthew 28:16-20. Why do you think this Scripture passage is often called "The Great Commission?"

According to this Scripture, what are the important elements of the Great Commission?

Read Acts 1:8. Do you think this verse applies to us today?

According to this verse, who empowers us to go and share the Good News?

The Bible tells us that Philip was an evangelist (see Acts 21:8). Read Acts 8:4-8 and describe the actions of Philip and the actions of the crowd.

The job of an evangelist is not to nurture Christians, but rather to preach to unbelievers the message of salvation in Christ.
In the following verses what was Philip's message?

Acts 8:12 _____

Acts 8:35 _____

THE GIFT OF PROPHECY

When the word "prophet" is spoken, we often think of the predictions of future events, fortune-telling, predicting the outcome of a football game or some other form of gaining information that was previously unknown to us.

The Old Testament prophets acted as God's mouthpiece for speaking His message to kings, common people and entire nations. The messages they spoke usually pertained to future events. In the New Testament and in recent history, prophecy, which in Greek means "to speak forth," usually had a different meaning. In the church, the gift of prophecy is the ability to "speak forth" or "proclaim" God's truth and how that truth applies to our everyday life.

"But one who prophesies, preaching the messages of God, is helping others grow in the Lord, encouraging and comforting them" (1 Corinthians 14:3, TLB).

According to the following Scriptures, what seems to be the primary job of a New Testament prophet?
(1 Corinthians 14:3)

SHARING
THE GOOD NEWS

HECK IT OUT

THE GIFT OF EVANGELISM/THE GIFT OF PROPHECY

The Gift of Evangelism
On a scale of 1-10 rate your responses to these statements:

1	2	3	4	5	6	7	8	9	10
NO		rarely		maybe			sometimes		YES!

.... I can tell nonbelievers about my relationship with Christ in a comfortable manner.

.... I always think of new ways in which I can share Christ with my non-Christian friends.

.... I have the ability to direct conversations toward the message of Christ.

.... I have led others to a personal relationship with Christ.

.... I desire to learn more about God so I can share Him in a clearer way.

.... I believe I have the gift of evangelism.

The Gift of Prophecy
On a scale of 1-10 rate your responses to these statements:

1	2	3	4	5	6	7	8	9	10
NO		rarely		maybe			sometimes		YES!

.... I have given others important messages at the perfect time that I felt came from God.

.... I believe I have the ability to reveal God's truth about the future.

.... I desire to speak messages from God that will challenge people to change.

.... I have had the chance to proclaim God's truth at the required time.

.... I have given messages that were judgments from God.

.... I believe I have the gift of prophecy.

TEAM EFFORT

THE LIFESAVING STATION[1]

On a dangerous seacoast where shipwrecks often occur there was once a crude little life-saving station. The building was just a hut, and there was only one boat but the few devoted members kept a constant watch over the sea, and with no thought for themselves went out day and night tirelessly searching for the lost. Some of those who were saved and various others in the surrounding area wanted to become associated with the station and give of their time, money and effort for the support of its work. New boats were bought and new crews trained. The little lifesaving station grew.

Some of the members of the lifesaving station were unhappy that the building was so crude and poorly equipped. They felt that a more comfortable place should be provided as the first refuge for those saved from the sea. They replaced the emergency cots with beds and put better furniture in the enlarged building. Now the lifesaving station became a popular gathering place for its members, and they decorated it beautifully and furnished it exquisitely because they used it as a sort of club. Fewer members were now interested in going to sea on lifesaving missions, so they hired lifeboat crews to do this work. The lifesaving motif still prevailed in this club's decoration and there was a liturgical lifeboat in the room where the club initiations were held. About this time a large ship was wrecked off the coast, and the hired crews brought in boat loads of cold, wet and half-drowned people. They were dirty and sick and some of them had black skin and some had yellow skin. The beautiful new club was in chaos. So the property committee immediately had a shower house built outside the club where victims of shipwreck could be cleaned up before coming inside.

At the next meeting, there was a split in the club membership. Most of the members wanted to stop the club's lifesaving activities because they were unpleasant and a hindrance to the normal social life of the club. Some members insisted upon lifesaving as their primary purpose and pointed out that they were still called a lifesaving station. But they were finally voted down and told that if they wanted to save lives of all the various kinds of people who were shipwrecked in those waters, they could begin their own lifesaving station down the coast. They did.

As the years went by, the new station experienced the same changes that had occurred in the old. It evolved into a club, and yet another lifesaving station was founded. History continued to repeat itself, and if you visit that seacoast today, you will find a number of exclusive clubs along that shore. Shipwrecks are frequent in those waters, but most of the people drown.

1. When was the lifesaving station most effective?

2. Where did the lifesaving station go wrong?

3. How is the church like a lifesaving station?

What is the purpose of the church?

4. How can the church and this youth group do a better job of evangelism?

1. Source unknown.

IN THE WORD

THE GIFT OF EVANGELISM/THE GIFT OF PROPHECY

The Gift of Evangelism

The word "evangelist" appears only three times in the entire New Testament (Acts 21:8; Ephesians 4:11, and 2 Timothy 4:5). In Ephesians 4:11 we read, "He gave some to be...evangelists." Though the word isn't used many times, its meaning is clearly defined. It means "one who proclaims the Good News."

Read Matthew 28:16-20. Why do you think this Scripture passage is often called "The Great Commission?"

According to this Scripture, what are the important elements of the Great Commission?

Read Acts 1:8. Do you think this verse applies to us today?

According to this verse, who empowers us to go and share the Good News?

The Bible tells us that Philip was an evangelist (see Acts 21:8). Read Acts 8:4-8 and describe the actions of Philip and the actions of the crowd.

The job of an evangelist is not to nurture Christians but rather to preach to unbelievers the message of salvation in Christ.

In the following verses what was Philip's message?

Acts 8:12

Acts 8:35

The Gift of Prophecy

When the word "prophet" is spoken, we often think of predictions of future events, fortune-telling, predicting the outcome of a football game or some other form of gaining truth that was previously unknown to us.

IN THE WORD

The Old Testament prophets acted as God's mouthpiece for speaking His message to kings, common people and entire nations. The messages they spoke usually pertained to future events. In the New Testament and in recent history, prophecy, which in Greek means "to speak forth," usually had a different meaning. In the church the gift of prophecy is the ability to "speak forth" or "proclaim" God's truth and how that truth applies to our everyday life.

"But one who prophesies, preaching the messages of God, is helping others grow in the Lord, encouraging and comforting them" (1 Corinthians 14:3, *TLB*).

According to the following Scriptures, what seems to be the primary job of a New Testament prophet?

1 Corinthians 14:3

_____

_____

Acts 15:32

_____

_____

Read Acts 13:1-5. What were the responsibilities of Barnabas and Saul?

_____

_____

Paul stresses the importance of the gift of prophecy in 1 Corinthians 14:1-5,39. Read these verses. Why do you think Paul views prophecy as being so important?

_____

_____

What issues do you think a person with the gift of prophecy would speak on in the present day?

_____

_____

So What?

Do you know someone who has the gift of prophecy? If so, how does he or she make you feel when you hear him or her speak?

_____

_____

*T*HINGS TO *T*HINK *A*BOUT

1. What makes sharing our faith (evangelism) often a scary experience?

....

....

....

2. What makes the Christian faith attractive to nonbelievers?

....

....

....

What makes it *not* attractive?

....

....

....

3. Who is a modern-day prophet in your opinion and why?

....

....

....

PARENT PAGE

OPERATION EVANGELIZE

"Therefore go and make disciples of all nations, baptizing them in the name of the Father and of the Son and of the Holy Spirit, and teaching them to obey everything I have commanded you. And surely I am with you always, to the very end of the age" (Matthew 28:19,20).

Here's a chance as a family to share your faith with others.

According to the Great Commission, who is called to evangelize?

....

....

....

What could hinder you from sharing the good news?

....

....

According to church growth experts, 25 percent of the people who do not attend church would come with you if you invited them!

Who can your family invite to church next week?

....

....

....

Operation Evangelize List

Name	What We Can Do to Share Our Faith

Pray for those people and get started.

Session 9 "Sharing the Good News"
Date ....

BUILDING UP THE CHURCH

K EY VERSES

"We have different gifts, according to the grace given us. If a man's gift is prophesying, let him use it in proportion to his faith. If it is serving, let him serve; if it is teaching, let him teach." Romans 12:6,7

"It was he who gave some to be apostles, some to be prophets, some to be evangelists, and some to be pastors and teachers." Ephesians 4:11

B IBLICAL BASIS

John 10:11-16; 21:16;
Acts 20:28;
Romans 12:6,7;
Ephesians 4:11;
2 Timothy 2:2;
Hebrews 13:20;
James 3:1;
1 Peter 2:25

T HE BIG IDEA

The church is built up by people who have the gifts of teaching and pastoring. These gifts help the Body of Christ grow spiritually.

A IMS OF THIS SESSION

During this session you will guide students to:

- Examine the spiritual gifts of teaching and pastoring;
- Discover and identify these specific gifts and consider their roles in the lives of others;
- Implement seeking these gifts or supporting those who have one of these gifts.

C HECK IT OUT

THE GIFT OF TEACHING/THE GIFT OF PASTORING—

Students rate their aptitudes in the gifts of teaching and pastoring.

T EAM EFFORT— JUNIOR HIGH/ MIDDLE SCHOOL

FAVORITE TEACHER SURVEY—

Students describe special teachers.

T EAM EFFORT— HIGH SCHOOL

ASK AND INTERVIEW—

An opportunity to interview the pastor.

I N THE WORD

THE GIFT OF TEACHING/THE GIFT OF PASTORING—

A Bible study exploring the various aspects of teaching and pastoring.

T HINGS TO THINK ABOUT (OPTIONAL)

Questions to get students thinking and talking about the qualities and requirements for teachers and pastors.

P ARENT PAGE

A tool to get the session into the home and allow parents and young people to discuss ways to support the pastor.

LEADER'S DEVOTIONAL

"And the things you have heard me say in the presence of many witnesses entrust to reliable men who will also be qualified to teach others" (2 Timothy 2:2).

Out of all the helpful and wonderful lessons I've learned from Jim Burns, the one lesson that has probably had the biggest impact on my life goes something like this: "Write down the 3-5 most influential sermons you've ever heard." When most people hear this, they struggle to recall three sermons they can even remember. Next, Jim says, "Okay, now write down the 3-5 most influential people in your life." People scribble furiously at this point.

The point is simple and obvious: People remember people; people rarely remember words. Though you may spend hours on message or lesson preparation, it's critical to remember that your students will remember you more than your words. Teaching is important, but your role as a pastor to your students puts your life and teaching in perspective. Your students don't want you to inspire them so much as they want you to encourage and listen to them. They want to know you care about them.

You are influencing the church of Jesus Christ for today and the next generation. Never forget that. Do you want students to remember your words or your life? Which will they remember? Will they really remember that Bible study on Babylonian license plate numbers? Teaching and learning the word of God is very important, but remembering a life is much easier than remembering someone's words. How many sermons can you remember? (Written by Joey O'Connor.)

"If you are not a disciple-maker, then I would suggest that you do the same thing that Timothy did with Paul, or that Peter, James, and John did with the Lord Jesus. Make yourself available to a disciple-maker who can help you to become a disciple-maker."—Walter Henrichsen

BUILDING UP THE CHURCH

🔑 KEY VERSES

"We have different gifts, according to the grace given us. If a man's gift is prophesying, let him use it in proportion to his faith. If it is serving, let him serve; if it is teaching, let him teach." Romans 12:6,7

"It was he who gave some to be apostles, some to be prophets, some to be evangelists, and some to be pastors and teachers." Ephesians 4:11

📖 BIBLICAL BASIS

John 10:11-16; 21:16; Acts 20:28; Romans 12:6,7; Ephesians 4:11; 2 Timothy 2:2; Hebrews 13:20; James 3:1; 1 Peter 2:25

⏱ THE BIG IDEA

The church is built up by people who have the gifts of teaching and pastoring. These gifts help the Body of Christ grow spiritually.

✓ CHECK IT OUT (5-10 MINUTES)

THE GIFT OF TEACHING/THE GIFT OF PASTORING

• Give each student a copy of "The Gift of Teaching/The Gift of Pastoring" on page 157 and a pen or pencil.

• Have students complete the page.

THE GIFT OF TEACHING

On a scale of 1-10 rate your responses to these statements:

1	2	3	4	5	6	7	8	9	10
NO		rarely		maybe			sometimes		YES!

_____ I enjoy explaining biblical truths to people.

_____ I think I have what it takes to teach a Bible study or lead a small group discussion.

_____ I am willing to spend extra time studying biblical principles in order to communicate them clearly to others.

_____ Because of my teaching, I have brought others to a better understanding of the Christian faith.

_____ Others tell me I present the gospel in a way that is easy to understand.

_____ I believe I have the gift of teaching.

SO WHAT?

How can you "pastor" your friends?

List three friends and some specific action you could take to shepherd, pastor and care for each of them this week.

My Friends   My Action Steps

1. _____

2. _____

3. _____

💭 THINGS TO THINK ABOUT (OPTIONAL)

• Use the questions on page 161 after or as a part of "In the Word."

1. What are some of the requirements for being a teacher of God's Word?

_____

2. What personal qualities do you think a pastor needs?

_____

3. Why is it that teaching and pastoring are such vulnerable positions in the church?

👪 PARENT PAGE

• Distribute page to parents.

THE GIFT OF PASTORING

On a scale of 1-10 rate your responses to these statements:

1	2	3	4	5	6	7	8	9	10
NO	rarely			maybe			sometimes		YES!

___ I have a way of relating to and comforting those who have fallen away from the Lord.

___ I try to know people in a personal way so that we feel comfortable with one another.

___ I would like the responsibilities that my pastor has.

___ I can see myself taking responsibility for the spiritual growth of others.

___ When I teach from the Bible my concern is that I see results in the spiritual growth of others.

___ I would like to be a pastor.

TEAM EFFORT—JUNIOR HIGH/MIDDLE SCHOOL (15-20 MINUTES)

FAVORITE TEACHER SURVEY

• Give each student a copy of "Favorite Teacher Survey" on page 159 and a pen or pencil, or display a copy using an overhead projector.

• Have the students complete the survey.

• Have a few students share about their favorite teachers.

Who are your favorite teachers (school, church, etc.) and what have you learned from them?

Teacher	Special Qualities	What I Learned
1.		
2.		
3.		

TEAM EFFORT—HIGH SCHOOL (15-20 MINUTES)

ASK AND INTERVIEW

• Arrange ahead of time for the pastor to visit the class for the first half of your class time.

• Give each student a 3 x 5 inch card. Ask the students to write down at least one question they would like to ask about the pastor's job.

• Allow the pastor to answer the written questions.

• If time allows, have the students ask more questions.

• Option: If the pastor is not available, invite a retired pastor or a pastor from another church.

THE GIFT OF TEACHING/THE GIFT OF PASTORING

THE GIFT OF TEACHING

• Divide students into groups of three or four.

Fold

• Give each student a copy of "In the Word" on pages 161 and 163 and a pen or pencil, or display a copy using an overhead projector.

• Have students complete the Bible study.

There are some teachers who have a remarkable impact on our lives. Usually it is not so much *what* they teach as *how* they teach. These teachers have been given a special gift to make spiritual truth and other subjects come alive. Many of these teachers have used this gift to greatly influence our lives.

"So we are to use our different gifts in accordance with the grace that God has given us...If it is to teach, we must teach" (Romans 12:6,7, *TEV*).

Brainstorm all the different types of teaching situations you can think of. (examples: large groups, regular school, Sunday school, one-on-one, writing, etc.)

___

Now circle the ones you feel most comfortable with.

Read and paraphrase James 3:1.

___

Why do you think the words of James 3:1 are so harsh?

___

THE GIFT OF PASTORING

"And his gifts were that some should be...pastors" (Ephesians 4:11, *RSV*). "Pastor" is the Latin word for "shepherd."

Read John 10:11-16. What qualities of a shepherd are described in this parable of Jesus?

___

If you were a shepherd, what would be your main responsibility?

___

What did Jesus mean when He said to Peter, "Take care of my sheep" (John 21:16)?

___

What else does the Bible say about the act of shepherding? Read the following Scriptures and next to the verse write the key words or phrases that lead to a better understanding of shepherding.

Acts 20:28 ___

Hebrews 13:20 ___

1 Peter 2:25 ___

Can you see how the New Testament portrays the shepherd as the person who cares for the flock and leads them into safe places? If the sheep wander away, the shepherd seeks them out and saves them. He protects them from their enemies.

How would you define "pastor" with the idea of a shepherd in mind?

**BUILDING UP
THE CHURCH**

 **HECK IT OUT**

THE GIFT OF TEACHING/THE GIFT OF PASTORING

The Gift of Teaching

On a scale of 1-10 rate your responses to these statements:

1	2	3	4	5	6	7	8	9	10
NO		rarely		maybe			sometimes		YES!

.... I enjoy explaining biblical truths to people.

.... I think I have what it takes to teach a Bible study or lead a small group discussion.

.... I am willing to spend extra time studying biblical principles in order to communicate them clearly to others.

.... Because of my teaching, I have brought others to a better understanding of the Christian faith.

.... Others tell me I present the gospel in a way that is easy to understand.

.... I believe I have the gift of teaching.

The Gift of Pastoring

On a scale of 1-10 rate your responses to these statements:

1	2	3	4	5	6	7	8	9	10
NO		rarely		maybe			sometimes		YES!

.... I have a way of relating to and comforting those who have fallen away from the Lord.

.... I try to know people in a personal way so that we feel comfortable with one another.

.... I would like the responsibilities that my pastor has.

.... I can see myself taking responsibility for the spiritual growth of others.

.... When I teach from the Bible my concern is that I see results in the spiritual growth of others.

.... I would like to be a pastor.

BUILDING UP
THE CHURCH

FAVORITE TEACHER SURVEY

Who are your favorite teachers (school, church, etc.) and what did you learn from them?

Teacher	Special qualities	What I learned
1.		
2.		
3.		

IN THE WORD

BUILDING UP THE CHURCH

THE GIFT OF TEACHING/THE GIFT OF PASTORING

The Gift of Teaching

There are some teachers who have a remarkable impact on our lives. Usually it is not so much *what* they teach as *how* they teach. These teachers have been given a special gift to make spiritual truth and other subjects come alive. Many of these teachers have used this gift to greatly influence our lives.

"So we are to use our different gifts in accordance with the grace that God has given us....If it is to teach, we must teach" (Romans 12:6,7, *TEV*).

Brainstorm all the different types of teaching situations you can think of.

Now circle the ones you feel most comfortable with.

Read and paraphrase James 3:1

Why do you think the words of James 3:1 are so harsh?

The Gift of Pastoring

"And his gifts were that some should be...pastors" (Ephesians 4:11, *RSV*). "Pastor" is the Latin word for shepherd.

Read John 10:11-16. What qualities of a shepherd are described in this parable of Jesus?

If you were a shepherd, what would be your main responsibility?

What did Jesus mean when He said to Peter, "Take care of my sheep" (John 21:16)?

What else does the Bible say about the act of shepherding? Read the following Scriptures and next to the verse write the key words or phrases that lead to a better understanding of shepherding.

Acts 20:28

Hebrews 13:20

1 Peter 2:25

IN THE WORD

Can you see how the New Testament portrays the shepherd as the person who cares for the flock and leads them into safe places? If the sheep wander away the shepherd seeks them out and saves them. He protects them from their enemies.

How would you define "pastor" with the idea of a shepherd in mind?

....

....

SO WHAT?
How can you "pastor" your friends?

....

....

List three friends and some specific action you could take to shepherd, pastor and care for each of them this week.

My Friends	My Action Steps
1.	
2.	
3.	

THINGS TO THINK ABOUT

1. **What are some of the requirements for being a teacher of God's Word?**

....

....

2. **What personal qualities do you think a pastor or teacher needs?**

....

....

3. **Why is it that teaching and pastoring are such vulnerable positions in the church?**

....

....

PARENT PAGE

A FAMILY BRAINSTORM

Who have been influential teachers in your life?

....

....

....

What are some situations when your family might need the pastor?

....

....

Pastor Johnson

Pastor Johnson is a wonderful person. You enjoy his fun-loving personality and his commitment to God. Lately he is looking very tired and discouraged. You know he is struggling with some of the leaders in the church, and giving has been down. You just heard that his daughter was caught stealing at the local mall. What can you do as a family to serve Pastor Johnson?

....

....

....

What do you think are the special needs of pastors?

....

....

....

As a family, what will you do in the next week and/or month to help or encourage your pastor?

....

....

....

Session 10 "Building Up the Church"

Date ....

KNOWING WHERE TO GO

KEY VERSES

"If it is encouraging, let him encourage; if it is contributing to the needs of others, let him give generously; if it is leadership, let him govern diligently; if it is showing mercy, let him do it cheerfully."
Romans 12:8

"And in the church God has appointed first of all apostles, second prophets, third teachers, then workers of miracles, also those having gifts of healing, those able to help others, those with gifts of administration, and those speaking in different kinds of tongues."
1 Corinthians 12:28

BIBLICAL BASIS

Exodus 18:13-27;
Matthew 7:22;
Mark 10:35-45;
Acts 4:37; 9:27;
Romans 12:6,8;
1 Corinthians 12:28;
Philippians 2:19-22;
1 Timothy 4:12; 6:14;
2 Timothy 2:22-26; 4:6,7

THE BIG IDEA

The Body of Christ needs certain women and men who have the gifts of leadership and administration to help steer and direct others to actions with positive results.

AIMS OF THIS SESSION

During this session you will guide students to:
• Examine the spiritual gifts of leadership and administration;
• Discover how these two gifts are vital to the health of the church;
• Implement how they can better develop these qualities in their lives.

CHECK IT OUT

THE GIFT OF LEADERSHIP /THE GIFT OF ADMINISTRATION—
Students rate their aptitudes in the the gifts of leadership and administration.

TEAM EFFORT— JUNIOR HIGH/ MIDDLE SCHOOL

A BOSS OR A LEADER?—
An activity to differentiate between a boss and a leader.

TEAM EFFORT— HIGH SCHOOL

YEARLY PLANNING SURVEY—
A questionnaire to aid in planning activities for the future.

IN THE WORD

THE GIFT OF LEADERSHIP/ THE GIFT OF ADMINISTRATION—
A Bible study exploring the various aspects of leading and administrating.

THINGS TO THINK ABOUT (OPTIONAL)

Questions to get students thinking and talking about the roles of leaders and administrators.

PARENT PAGE

A tool to get the session into the home and allow parents and young people to discuss leadership qualities.

LEADER'S DEVOTIONAL

"Many will say to me on that day, 'Lord, Lord, did we not prophesy in your name, and in your name drive out demons and perform many miracles?'" (Matthew 7:22).

If you've spent any time in the super bookstores lately, you'll notice that the leadership and business management sections are booming. Every day, more and more books come out on leadership development, leadership strategy, empowerment, re-engineering and personal success. If you take the message of some of these books and compare them to God's plan for leadership development found in the Bible, you'll see some crucial differences.

Popular Leadership Books Say	God Says
"Be powerful!"	"Be humble."
"Take charge!"	"Submit."
"Be in control!"	"Give up control."
"Rule with an iron fist."	"Serve in love."
"Win at all costs!"	"Count the cost."

Jesus Christ is asking his followers to walk with him in a completely different style of leadership and obedience. God wants you to administer His kingdom—not the kingdom of man. Leadership without an authentic love for God is hollow. Christian leadership without servanthood is hypocrisy.

Most people don't want to be led, but they are willing to be served. You have the opportunity to show students a different way: The way of God; the way of the Cross. Students will eagerly walk with an honest, authentic person who serves others before him or herself. You can show your students Jesus' design for following Him. Use this lesson to explore how you can be servant leaders of Jesus in order to administer His kingdom here on earth. (Written by Joey O'Connor.)

"He who cannot obey, cannot command."—Benjamin Franklin

KNOWING WHERE TO GO

EY VERSES

"If it is encouraging, let him encourage; if it is contributing to the needs of others, let him give generously; if it is leadership, let him govern diligently; if it is showing mercy, let him do it cheerfully." Romans 12:8

"And in the church God has appointed first of all apostles, second prophets, third teachers, then workers of miracles, also those having gifts of healing, those able to help others, those with gifts of administration, and those speaking in different kinds of tongues."
1 Corinthians 12:28

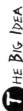IBLICAL BASIS

Exodus 18:13-27; Matthew 7:22; Mark 10:35-45; Acts 4:37; 9:27; Romans 12:6,8; 1 Corinthians 12:28; Philippians 2:19-22; 1 Timothy 4:12; 6:14; 2 Timothy 2:22-26; 4:6,7

The BIG IDEA

The Body of Christ needs women and men who have the gifts of leadership and administration to help steer and direct others to actions with positive results.

HECK IT OUT (5-10 MINUTES)

• Give each student a copy of "The Gift of Leadership/The Gift of Administration" on page 171 and a pen or pencil.
• Have students complete the page.

THE GIFT OF LEADERSHIP/THE GIFT OF ADMINISTRATION

THE GIFT OF LEADERSHIP
On a scale of 1-10 rate your responses to these statements:

1	2	3	4	5	6	7	8	9	10
NO		rarely		maybe		sometimes			YES!

_____ I believe I know where I am going (and other people seem to follow).

_____ I would enjoy leading, inspiring and motivating others to become involved in God's work.

_____ I want to lead people to the best solution when they have troubles.

_____ I have influenced others to complete a task or to find a biblical answer that helped their lives.

What should the words "leader" and "servant" mean to a Christian?

How does this differ from the meaning the world attaches to these words?

THE GIFT OF ADMINISTRATION
How does this differ from the gift of leadership?

A _____ could be thought of as a quarterback who helps the football team score a touchdown while the _____ is like a coach who designs the plays for the quarterback to run.
The visit by Jethro to his son-in-law Moses is recorded in Exodus 18. Jethro used his gift of administration to greatly help the ministry of Moses. Read Exodus 18:13-27. What advice did Jethro give to Moses?

How did this advice affect the life and work of Moses?

What could someone with the gift of administration do to help
The youth group?

The church?

Can a leader also have the gift of administration? Explain.

What positive steps should the leader take if he or she doesn't have the gift of administration?

So WHAT?
How can you develop better leadership or administrative qualities in your life?

THINGS TO THINK ABOUT (OPTIONAL)
• Use the questions on page 187 after or as a part of "In the Word."
1. Why is it that we often do not associate the term "leader" with "servant"?

2. In what ways was Jesus a leader to His disciples?

To the crowds?

To His enemies?

3. If someone didn't like to be in front of a group, could he or she still have the gift of leadership or administration?

PARENT PAGE
• Distribute page to parents.

_____ When I'm in a group, I'm usually the leader or I take the lead if no one else does.

_____ I believe I have leadership skills.

THE GIFT OF ADMINISTRATION

On a scale of 1-10 rate your responses to these statements:

1   2   3   4   5   6   7   8   9   10

NO   rarely   maybe   sometimes   YES!

_____ I see clearly that a job can be done more effectively if I allow others to assist.

_____ I would enjoy directing a vacation Bible school, recreation program, or special event for my church.

_____ I can give others responsibilities for a task or project and help them accomplish it.

_____ I am able to set goals and plan the most effective way to reach them.

_____ I believe I have the gift of administration.

TEAM EFFORT—JUNIOR HIGH/MIDDLE SCHOOL (15-20 MINUTES)

A BOSS OR A LEADER?

• Give each student a copy of the "A Boss or a Leader?" on pages 171 and 173 and a pen or pencil, or display a copy using an overhead projector.

• Have students complete the first step only. When everyone is finished, quickly review the results by reading through each phrase or sentence and asking: Do you think this describes a boss or a leader?

• Then have students do the second step, which involves a personal evaluation. After several minutes, have them form pairs and complete the following sentences aloud:

1. The one characteristic I most need to eliminate from my life is:

2. The one characteristic I most need to add to my life is:

3. One positive trait from the list that I see in you is:

After students have shared, have them pray together, committing to work on adding to their lives the characteristic they said they most needed.

TEAM EFFORT—HIGH SCHOOL (15-20 MINUTES)

YEARLY PLANNING SURVEY

• Give each student a copy of the "Yearly Planning Survey" on pages 177, 179 and 181 and a pen or pencil.

• Allow time for students to complete the survey, reminding them that their answers may remain anonymous if they wish.

• Surveys can often be very helpful in determining a group's needs and in evaluating your own ministry. This survey gets at four different areas: doctrinal understanding (questions 1-8), self-concept (questions 9-18), the youth group (questions 19-29), and personal spiritual growth (questions 30-39). Let the students know that you don't want their names—just their honest answers.

IN THE WORD (25-30 MINUTES)

THE GIFT OF LEADERSHIP/THE GIFT OF ADMINISTRATION

• Divide students into groups of three or four.

• Give each student a copy of "The Gift of Leadership/The Gift of Administration" on pages 183, 185 and 187 and a pen or pencil.

• Have students complete the Bible study.

THE GIFT OF LEADERSHIP

1 Timothy 4:12 _____

1 Timothy 6:14 _____

2 Timothy 2:22-26 _____

2 Timothy 4:6,7 _____

Read Philippians 2:19-22. How does Paul describe Timothy to the Philippians? _____

"And since we have gifts that differ according to the grace given to us, let each exercise them accordingly...he who leads, with diligence" (Romans 12:6,8, NASB). The literal definition of a leader is one who "stands before" others. This means the gift of leadership is the special ability from God to set goals from God and then lead others to work together to carry out those goals for the glory of God. List a few qualities of a leader that would support this definition. _____

Jesus Christ gives us a perfect model of leadership. From what you know of the life of Jesus, can you recall specific times when Jesus used the gift of leadership? _____

Jesus appointed, trained and led 12 apostles who, after His death, became the leaders of the early church (see Acts 4:31; 9:27). During Christ's time with these apostles, He taught them many things, including leadership. Two of Christ's apostles, James and John, asked Him an interesting question. Read Mark 10:35-41. What was their question? _____

Do you think they asked that question because:

1. They always wanted to be close to Jesus?

2. They thought since they were leaders they should be first in God's kingdom?

3. They thought those were the best seats in the "house"?

4. Other: _____

Explain your answer. _____

Let's see how Jesus responded to their question:

"So Jesus called them all together to him and said: 'You know that the men who are considered rulers of the people have power over them, and the leaders rule over them. This, however, is not the way it is among you. If one of you wants to be great, he must be the servant of the rest; and if one of you wants to be first, he must be the slave of all. For even the Son of Man did not come to be served; he came to serve and give his life to redeem many people'" (Mark 10:42-45, TEV). What point is Jesus trying to make in these verses? _____

CHECK IT OUT

THE GIFT OF LEADERSHIP/THE GIFT OF ADMINISTRATION

The Gift of Leadership

On a scale of 1-10 rate your responses to these statements:

1	2	3	4	5	6	7	8	9	10
NO		rarely		maybe		sometimes			YES!

.... I believe I know where I am going (and other people seem to follow).

.... I would enjoy leading, inspiring and motivating others to become involved in God's work.

.... I want to lead people to the best solution when they have troubles.

.... I have influenced others to complete a task or to find a biblical answer that helped their lives.

.... When I'm in a group I'm usually the leader or I take the lead if no one else does.

.... I believe I have leadership skills.

The Gift of Administration

On a scale of 1-10 rate your responses to these statements:

1	2	3	4	5	6	7	8	9	10
NO		rarely		maybe		sometimes			YES!

.... I see clearly that a job can be done more effectively if I allow others to assist.

.... I would enjoy directing a vacation Bible school, recreation program, or special event for my church.

.... I can give others responsibilities for a task or project and help them accomplish it.

.... I am able to set goals and plan the most effective way to reach them.

.... I believe I have the gift of administration.

TEAM EFFORT

KNOWING
WHERE TO GO

A BOSS OR A LEADER?[1]

Do you think these statements describe a boss or a leader?

Step 1: In the first space before each of the following words or phrases, mark "B" if it describes a boss, or "L" if it describes a leader. No double answers allowed!

Step 2: In the second space before the following words or phrases, place a checkmark if it describes how you try to influence others. After you've placed all your checkmarks, compare how many "B" checkmarks you have versus "L" checkmarks to see what kind of a leader you are.

Step 1	Step 2	
		makes suggestions
		asks lots of questions
		demands obedience
		threatens
		likes the word "we"
		likes the word "I"
		assumes the worst
		pushes others
		encourages others
		coaches
		pesters
		assumes the best
		acts first, then asks others to follow
		makes assignments
		gives rewards
		gives orders
		persuades
		speaks bluntly
		shares the credit
		speaks first, then acts if needed
		complains
		emphasizes loyalty
		tries to be considerate
		punishes
		often says thanks
		uses fear
		keeps others guessing
		listens
		tries to be enthusiastic
		emphasizes position and title
		is task-oriented
		is person-oriented
		wins arguments

TEAM EFFORT

KNOWING WHERE TO GO

Number of Bs ....

Number of Ls ....

Characteristic from list you want to get rid of: ....

....

Characteristic from list you want to add: ....

Discussion Questions: Share your answers to the following questions with a partner.

The one characteristic I most need to eliminate from my life is:

....

The one characteristic I most need to add to my life is:

....

One positive trait from the list that I see in you is:

....

After you have shared, pray with your partner, committing to work on adding to your life the characteristic you said you most needed.

Note:

1. *Christlike Leadership*, Group Publishing (Loveland, CO: 1992) p. 32. Used by permission.

TEAM EFFORT

YEARLY PLANNING SURVEY[1]

KNOWING
WHERE TO GO

Make a check on the line which best represents your response to the following statements:

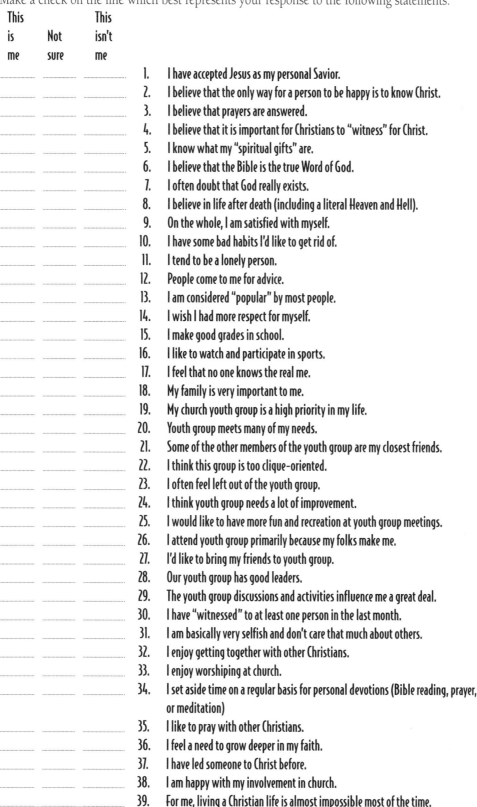

This is me	Not sure	This isn't me		
			1.	I have accepted Jesus as my personal Savior.
			2.	I believe that the only way for a person to be happy is to know Christ.
			3.	I believe that prayers are answered.
			4.	I believe that it is important for Christians to "witness" for Christ.
			5.	I know what my "spiritual gifts" are.
			6.	I believe that the Bible is the true Word of God.
			7.	I often doubt that God really exists.
			8.	I believe in life after death (including a literal Heaven and Hell).
			9.	On the whole, I am satisfied with myself.
			10.	I have some bad habits I'd like to get rid of.
			11.	I tend to be a lonely person.
			12.	People come to me for advice.
			13.	I am considered "popular" by most people.
			14.	I wish I had more respect for myself.
			15.	I make good grades in school.
			16.	I like to watch and participate in sports.
			17.	I feel that no one knows the real me.
			18.	My family is very important to me.
			19.	My church youth group is a high priority in my life.
			20.	Youth group meets many of my needs.
			21.	Some of the other members of the youth group are my closest friends.
			22.	I think this group is too clique-oriented.
			23.	I often feel left out of the youth group.
			24.	I think youth group needs a lot of improvement.
			25.	I would like to have more fun and recreation at youth group meetings.
			26.	I attend youth group primarily because my folks make me.
			27.	I'd like to bring my friends to youth group.
			28.	Our youth group has good leaders.
			29.	The youth group discussions and activities influence me a great deal.
			30.	I have "witnessed" to at least one person in the last month.
			31.	I am basically very selfish and don't care that much about others.
			32.	I enjoy getting together with other Christians.
			33.	I enjoy worshiping at church.
			34.	I set aside time on a regular basis for personal devotions (Bible reading, prayer, or meditation)
			35.	I like to pray with other Christians.
			36.	I feel a need to grow deeper in my faith.
			37.	I have led someone to Christ before.
			38.	I am happy with my involvement in church.
			39.	For me, living a Christian life is almost impossible most of the time.

 **TEAM EFFORT**

KNOWING WHERE TO GO

Strengths of our youth group: ....

....

Weaknesses of our youth group: ....

....

Please check five of the following activities that you would like to see our youth group do in the near future:

.... Beach party	.... Bike trip
.... Tubing party	.... Trip to different colleges
.... Halloween party	.... Weekend retreat
.... Movie night	.... Summer camp
.... Camping trip	.... Youth week
.... Have a dance	.... Youth-led worship
.... Hay ride	.... Put on a play
.... Go to a ball game	.... Have a Christian concert
.... Go to an amusement park	.... Go to a concert
.... Water-skiing trip	.... Service project of some kind
.... Lock-in	.... Have a fund-raiser
.... Bowling	.... Have a work camp
.... Roller/ice skating	.... Car rally
.... Progressive dinner	.... Other: _____

Subjects I would like to see discussed in our group:

1=a must   2= maybe   3= not interested

.... Sex	.... Making my life count for the Lord
.... Fasting	.... How to study the Bible
.... Holy Spirit	.... Worship
.... Disciples	.... Books of the Bible
.... Temptation	.... Lifestyle assessment
.... Guilt	.... Church
.... Worry/depression	.... Ethics
.... Temper	.... Abortion
.... Tongues	.... Death and dying
.... Satan	.... Euthanasia
.... Fruit of the Spirit	.... Divorce
.... Doubt	.... Pacifism
.... Prayer	.... Stewardship
.... Sin	.... Basics of the faith
.... Introduction to the New Testament	.... Love
.... Humility	.... Missions
.... Obedience	.... Other faiths
.... Spiritual gifts	.... Parent/child relationships
.... Rock music	.... Dating

 **TEAM EFFORT**

 KNOWING WHERE TO GO

Spiritual battles	Witnessing
Revelation	Authority, government
Genesis	Servanthood
Love or infatuation	Prejudice
Walking in the light	Self-acceptance
Who's who in the Bible	Nuclear power
Communication skills	Relationships
Family	Materialism
Life of Christ	Peer pressure
Christian apologetics	Sermon on the Mount
Stress	Perseverance
Forgiveness	Psalms
Walk your talk	Proverbs
Gossip	Prophecy
Community	Current events
Friendships	Career
Environmental responsibilities	Evolution
Balanced lifestyle	End times
Discipline	Philosophy
Body life	Christian vocations
Heaven	Homosexuality
Introduction to the Old Testament	Body as God's temple
Drinking	Preparing for college
Tough questions	Ministry/calling
Law	Assurance of salvation
Commandments	Cost of commitment
Paul's missionary journeys	Fellowship

Note:

1. *Ideas Number 21-24* (El Cajon, CA: Youth Specialties, 1984) pp. 112,113. Used by permission.

IN THE WORD

THE GIFT OF LEADERSHIP/THE GIFT OF ADMINISTRATION

The Gift of Leadership

Many times when we hear the word "leader" we think of an authority figure standing above everyone else. He or she might have an outgoing personality or the ability to speak well in front of groups. But these qualities do not always make a person a good leader. Even if you are shy and timid, you may have real leadership ability. Perhaps you are a leader but you've never realized it.

To help shatter some of our misconceptions, let's take a look at Paul's letters to Timothy. Notice how Paul encouraged Timothy in the following verses. After each verse, find the advice that Paul gave to Timothy concerning Timothy's leadership.

1 Timothy 4:12

1 Timothy 6:14

2 Timothy 2:22-26

2 Timothy 4:6,7

Read Philippians 2:19-22. How does Paul describe Timothy to the Philippians?

"And since we have gifts that differ according to the grace given to us, let each exercise them accordingly...he who leads, with diligence" (Romans 12:6,8, *NASB*).

The literal definition of a leader is one who "stands before" others. This means the gift of leadership is the special ability from God to set goals from God and then lead others to work together to carry out those goals for the glory of God.

List a few qualities of a leader that would support this definition.

Jesus Christ gives us a perfect model of leadership. From what you know of the life of Jesus, can you recall specific times when Jesus used the gift of leadership?

IN THE WORD

Jesus appointed, trained and led 12 apostles who, after His death, became the leaders of the early church (see Acts 4:37, 9:27). During Christ's time with these apostles, He taught them many things, including leadership. Two of Christ's apostles, James and John, asked Him an interesting question.

Read Mark 10:35-41. What was their question?

Do you think they asked that question because:
1. **They always wanted to be close to Jesus?**
2. **They thought since they were leaders they should be first in God's kingdom?**
3. **They thought those were the best seats in the "house"?**
4. **Other:**

Explain your answer.

Let's see how Jesus responded to their question:

"So Jesus called them all together to him and said: 'You know that the men who are considered rulers of the people have power over them, and the leaders rule over them. This, however, is not the way it is among you. If one of you wants to be great, he must be the servant of the rest; and if one of you wants to be first, he must be the slave of all. For even the Son of Man did not come to be served; he came to serve and give his life to redeem many people'" (Mark 10:42-45, *TEV*).

What point is Jesus trying to make in these verses?

What should the words "leader" and "servant" mean to a Christian?

How does this differ from the meaning the world attaches to these words?

The Gift of Administration

The gift of administration is very similar to the gift of leadership. These gifts have been described as different from each other, but they are related. The difference is that leadership is defined by what a person *is* while administration is defined by what the person *does*.

IN THE WORD

"And God has appointed in the church...administrators" (1 Corinthians 12:28, *RSV*). The Greek word Paul used that has been translated "administrators" is a graphic word that literally refers to the work of a helmsman or pilot (captain) who steers a ship through rocks and sandbars to safe harbor.

The gift of administration is the special ability that God gives to certain members of the Body of Christ which helps them to clearly understand the present and future goals of a group. People with the gift of administration are able to plan workable ways to reach these goals.

How does this differ from the gift of leadership?

....

....

A .... could be thought of as a quarterback who helps the football team score a touchdown while the .... is like a coach who designs the plays for the quarterback to run.

The visit by Jethro to his son-in-law Moses is recorded in Exodus 18. Jethro used his gift of administration to greatly help the ministry of Moses. Read Exodus 18:13-27. What advice did Jethro give to Moses?

....

....

How did this advice affect the life and work of Moses?

....

....

What could someone with the gift of administration do to help:

Your youth group? ....

....

Your church? ....

....

Can a leader also have the gift of administration? Explain.

....

....

What positive steps should the leader take if he or she doesn't have the gift of administration?

....

....

SO WHAT?
How can you develop better leadership or administrative qualities in your life?

....

....

THINGS TO THINK ABOUT

1. Why is it that we often do not associate the term "leader" with "servant"?

....

....

....

2. In what ways was Jesus a leader to His disciples?

....

....

....

   To the crowds?

....

....

....

   To His enemies?

....

....

....

3. If someone doesn't like to be in front of a group, could he or she still have the gift of leadership or administration?

....

....

....

PARENT PAGE

KNOWING WHERE TO GO

MOST ADMIRED LIST

List the top five people on your "Most Admired" list and share what you admire about them.

Name	What I Admire
1.	
2.	
3.	
4.	
5.	

Complete the following sentences.

The greatest leader in the history of our world is/was...

These qualities are a must for leadership...

Now share the positive leadership qualities you see in each family member.

Session 11 "Knowing Where to Go"

Date

SPIRITUAL GIFTS DISCOVERY

INSTRUCTIONS

Step 1   Go through the list of 120 statements in the questionnaire on pages 195-201. For each one, mark on the Answer Sheet to what extent the statement is true of your life: MUCH, SOME, LITTLE, or NOT AT ALL.

Step 2   After filling in your scores, transfer the names of the spiritual gifts to their corresponding rows. The highest scores may indicate you have the corresponding gifts. You will want to refer to the gift definitions and Scripture references you've previously studied.

LEADER'S DEVOTIONAL

"Not that we are competent in ourselves to claim anything for ourselves, but our competence comes from God. He has made us competent as ministers of a new covenant—not of the letter but of the Spirit; for the letter kills, but the Spirit gives life" (2 Corinthians 3:5,6).

As you close this study on spiritual gifts, don't forget the greatest spiritual gift of all—Jesus Christ. Jesus has first and foremost called you to a growing, deepening relationship with Him. He hasn't called you to a spectacular program that draws hundreds of teenagers, a concert series, a Bible study, a hilarious crowdbreaker game or a lock-in. He hasn't even called you to be the greatest youth worker in the world. Or even the greatest youth worker in Pokamoko, Missouri.

God doesn't want you to depend on your spiritual gifts, talents, abilities, passions, personality, looks or unique skills to perform stupid youth worker tricks. God has called you to depend on Him. That's something I too easily forget. I hope you're not as forgetful as me, but if you are, we have a God full of mercy, grace, forgiveness and every other spiritual gift imaginable. His heart's desire is for us to depend on Him. With the spiritual gifts and blessings He's given us, He wants to work through our lives for His purpose.

Being dependent on God is a great way to show your love and appreciation for God. As you depend on Him in every situation you encounter, you will model to your students a life devoted to God. What students want and need most is to see God at work in your life. They don't want to see your spiritual gifts as much as they want to see God in action. Before you begin this lesson on discovering your spiritual gifts, why not spend some time with the greatest spiritual gift of all? (Written by Joey O'Connor.)

"God has also designed the gifts to help 'unite' the body of Christ... thus the gifts of the Spirit should never divide the body of Christ; they should unify it."—Billy Graham

SPIRITUAL GIFTS DISCOVERY

1. I could be described as an "others-centered" person.
2. I believe I have the gift of helping.
3. I enjoy giving hope to those in need.
4. When people are in need I enjoy having them in my home. I do not feel like they are intruding.
5. I believe I have a prayer language which is in a tongue unknown to me.
6. God has used me in a supernatural way to heal someone.
7. I believe I have the gift of exhortation.
8. I see myself as a person who is very generous when it comes to giving money to my church.
9. My friends view me as a person who is wise.
10. I have expressed thoughts of truth that have given insight to others.
11. I often feel I know God's will even when others aren't sure.
12. I would like to be a missionary.
13. I can tell nonbelievers about my relationship with Christ in a comfortable manner.
14. I have given others important messages that I felt came from God at the perfect time.
15. I enjoy explaining biblical truths to people.
16. I have a way of relating to and comforting those who have fallen away from the Lord.
17. I believe I know where I am going and other people seem to follow.
18. I see clearly that a job can be done more effectively if I allow others to assist.
19. Many incredible acts of God have happened to others through me.
20. There has been a time when I heard someone speak in an unknown language and I was able to interpret what he or she said.
21. I enjoy meeting the needs of others.
22. I'm the one who often cleans up after the meeting without being asked.
23. I believe I have the gift of mercy.
24. I enjoy having strangers in my home. I like making them feel comfortable.
25. I have spoken in tongues.
26. I have healed a physically disabled person.
27. I believe I have the ability to comfort those who are "off-track" and help them get back on track.
28. I believe I have the gift of giving.
29. I believe God has given me the ability to make wise decisions.
30. I desire fully to understand biblical truths.
31. I enjoy helping others with spiritual needs.
32. I feel comfortable when I'm around people of a different culture, race or language.
33. I believe I have the gift of evangelism.
34. I believe I have the ability to reveal God's truth about the future.
35. I think I have what it takes to teach a Bible study or lead a small group discussion.
36. I try to know people in a personal way so that we feel comfortable with one another.
37. I would enjoy leading, inspiring, and motivating others to become involved in God's work.

*S*PIRITUAL GIFTS DISCOVERY

38. I would enjoy directing a vacation Bible school, recreation program or special event for my church.
39. God has used me to specifically perform miraculous signs and wonders.
40. I believe I have the gift of interpretation of tongues.
41. You'll frequently find me volunteering my time to help with the needs of the church.
42. I seldom think twice before doing a task that might not bring me praise.
43. I would like to visit rest homes and other institutions where people need visitors.
44. I believe I have the gift of hospitality.
45. When I speak in tongues, I feel God's Spirit within me.
46. The gift of healing is evident in my life.
47. I have a desire to learn more about counseling so I can help others.
48. I have a strong desire to use my money wisely, knowing God will direct my giving.
49. I believe God has blessed me with the gift of wisdom.
50. I am able to help others understand God's Word.
51. I find it easy to trust God in difficult situations.
52. I adapt easily to a change of settings.
53. I have the ability to direct conversations toward the message of Christ.
54. I believe I have the gift of prophecy.
55. I am willing to spend extra time studying biblical principles in order to communicate them clearly to others.
56. I would like the responsibilities that my pastor has.
57. I want to lead people to the best solution when they have troubles.
58. I can give others responsibilities for a task or project and help them accomplish it.
59. God has performed humanly impossible miracles through my life.
60. God has shown me what someone is saying when he or she is speaking in tongues.
61. I'm the type of person that likes to reach out to less fortunate people.
62. I receive joy doing jobs that others see as "thankless."
63. I am very compassionate to those in need.
64. I believe God has given me the ability to make others feel comfortable in my home.
65. I believe I have the gift of tongues.
66. I have the ability to heal.
67. I have helped others in their struggles.
68. I am confident that God will take care of my needs when I give sacrificially and cheerfully.
69. I feel confident that my decisions are in harmony with God's will.
70. I believe I have the gift of knowledge.
71. I trust in God for supernatural miracles.

SPIRITUAL GIFTS DISCOVERY

72. I have a strong desire to see people in other countries won to the Lord.
73. I have led others to a personal relationship with Christ.
74. I have had the chance to proclaim God's truth at the required time.
75. I believe I have the gift of teaching.
76. I would like to be a pastor.
77. I have influenced others to complete a task or to find a biblical answer that helped their lives.
78. I am able to set goals and plan the most effective way to reach them.
79. Others have mentioned to me that I was used by God to bring about a supernatural change in their lives.
80. I have been used to interpret tongues and Christ was glorified.
81. I feel good when I help with the routine jobs at the church.
82. I am able to do jobs that others won't do and I feel good about myself.
83. I have a desire to work with people who have special physical needs.
84. I want my house to always be a spot where people in need can come and find rest.
85. An unknown language comes to me when I'm at a loss for words in my prayer time.
86. God is glorified when He heals others through me.
87. I enjoy seeing people respond to encouragement.
88. I am a cheerful giver of my money.
89. I usually see clear solutions to complicated problems.
90. I have the ability to learn new insights on my own.
91. I believe I have the gift of faith.
92. I am willing to go wherever God wants to send me.
93. I desire to learn more about God so I can share Him in a clearer way.
94. I have given messages that were judgments from God.
95. Others tell me I present the gospel in a way that is easy to understand.
96. When I teach from the Bible my concern is that I see results in the spiritual growth of others.
97. I believe I have leadership skills.
98. I enjoy learning about management issues and how organizations function.
99. I have witnessed God's miraculous power in and through my life.
100. I have interpreted tongues in such a way that it has blessed others.
101. I believe I have the gift of serving.
102. You'll often find me volunteering to do "behind the scenes" activities that few notice but must be done.
103. I would like to have a ministry with those who are needy.
104. I enjoy providing food and housing to those in need.
105. Others have interpreted my unknown prayer language.
106. I believe I have the gift of healing.
107. I am known for the way I encourage others.
108. I enjoy giving money to the needy.

SPIRITUAL GIFTS DISCOVERY

109. God has given me the ability to give clear counsel and advice to others.
110. I tend to use biblical insights when I share with others.
111. Others in my group see me as a faithful Christian.
112. I believe I could learn a new language well enough to minister to those in a different culture.
113. I always think of new ways in which I can share Christ with my non-Christian friends.
114. I desire to speak messages from God that will challenge people to change.
115. Because of my teaching, I have brought others to a better understanding of the Christian faith.
116. I can see myself taking responsibility for the spiritual growth of others.
117. When I'm in a group I'm usually the leader or I take the lead if no one else does.
118. I believe I have the gift of administration.
119. I believe I have the gift of miracles.
120. God has used my gift of interpretation of tongues to speak a message to the church.

SPIRITUAL
GIFTS DISCOVERY

ANSWER SHEET

In the grid below, enter the numerical value of each of your responses next to the number of the corresponding statement from the Spiritual Gifts Discovery.

MUCH=3   SOME=2   LITTLE=1   NOT AT ALL=0

Then add up the five numbers that you have recorded in each row and place the sum in the "total" column.

Rows	Value of Answers						Total	Gift
A	1	21	41	61	81	101		
B	2	22	42	62	82	102		
C	3	23	43	63	83	103		
D	4	24	44	64	84	104		
E	5	25	45	65	85	105		
F	6	26	46	66	86	106		
G	7	27	47	67	87	107		
H	8	28	48	68	88	108		
I	9	29	49	69	89	109		
J	10	30	50	70	90	110		
K	11	31	51	71	91	111		
L	12	32	52	72	92	112		
M	13	33	53	73	93	113		
N	14	34	54	74	94	114		
O	15	35	55	75	95	115		
P	16	36	56	76	96	116		
Q	17	37	57	77	97	117		
R	18	38	58	78	98	118		
S	19	39	59	79	99	119		
T	20	40	60	80	100	120		

A. Serving	B. Helping	C. Mercy	D. Hospitality
E. Tongues	F. Healing	G. Exhortation	H. Giving
I. Wisdom	J. Knowledge	K. Faith	L. Apostle and Missionary
M. Evangelism	N. Prophecy	O. Teaching	P. Pastoring
Q. Leadership	R. Administration	S. Miracles	T. Interpretation of Tongues

Add a New Member to Your Youth Staff.

Meet Jim Burns. He won't play guitar and he doesn't do windows, but he will take care of your programming needs. That's because his new curriculum, **YouthBuilders Group Bible Studies,** is a comprehensive program designed to take your group through their high school years. (If you have junior high kids in your group, **YouthBuilders** works for them too.)

Jim Burns is president of the National Institute of Youth Ministry.

For less than $6 a month, you'll get Jim Burns' special recipe of high-involvement, discussion-oriented, Bible-centered studies. It's the next generation of Bible curriculum for youth—and with Jim on your staff, you'll be free to spend more time one-on-one with the kids in your group.

Here are some of Youth-Builders' hottest features:

- Reproducible pages—one book fits your whole group
- Wide appeal—big groups, small groups—even adjusts to combine junior high/high school groups
- Hits home—special section to involve parents with every session of the study
- Interactive Bible discovery—geared to help young people find answers themselves
- Cheat sheets—a Bible *Tuck-In*™ with all the session information on a single page
- Flexible format—perfect for Sunday mornings, midweek youth meetings, or camps and retreats
- Three studies in one—each study has three four-session modules that examine critical life choices.

12 Books in the Series!

The Word on Sex, Drugs & Rock 'N' Roll
ISBN 08307.16424 $16.99

The Word on Prayer and the Devotional Life
ISBN 08307.16432 $16.99

The Word on the Basics of Christianity
ISBN 08307.16440 $16.99

The Word on Being a Leader, Serving Others & Sharing Your Faith
ISBN 08307.16459 $16.99

The Word on Helping Friends in Crisis
ISBN 08307.16467 $16.99

The Word on the Life of Jesus
ISBN 08307.16475 $16.99

The Word on Finding and Using Your Spiritual Gifts
ISBN 08307.17897 $16.99

The Word on the Sermon on the Mount
ISBN 08307.17234 $16.99

The Word on Spiritual Warfare
ISBN 08307.17242 $16.99

The Word on the New Testament
ISBN 08307.17250 $16.99

The Word on the Old Testament
ISBN 08307.17269 $16.99

The Word on Family
ISBN 08307.17277 $16.99

More Great Resources from Jim Burns

Drugproof Your Kids
Stephen Arterburn and Jim Burns

Solid biblical principles are combined with the most effective prevention and intervention techniques to give parents a guide they can trust.
ISBN 08307.17714 $10.99

Drugproof Your Kids Video
A 90-minute seminar featuring Stephen Arterburn and Jim Burns. Includes a reproducible syllabus.
SPCN 85116.00876 $19.99

Parenting Teens Positively
Video *Featuring Jim Burns*

Understand the forces shaping the world of a teenager and what you can do to be a positive influence. This powerful message of hope is for anyone working with—or living with—youth. Includes reproducible syllabus. UPC 607135.000655 $29.99

Surviving Adolescence
Jim Burns

Jim Burns helps teens—and their parents—negotiate the path from adolescence to adulthood with real-life stories that show how to make it through the teen years in one piece. ISBN 08307.20650 $9.99

For these and more great resources and to learn about NIYM's leadership training, call **1-800-397-9725.**

Gospel Light

FRESH IDEAS

RESOURCES FOR YOUTH WORKERS

Jim Burns, General Editor

Turn your youth group meetings into dynamic, exciting events that kids look forward to attending week after week! Supercharge your messages, grab their attention with your activities and connect with kids the first time and every time with these great resources. Just try to keep these books on the shelf!

ILLUSTRATIONS, STORIES AND QUOTES TO HANG YOUR MESSAGE ON

Few things get your point across faster or with greater impact than a memorable story with a twist. Grab your teens' attention by talking with your mouth full of unforgettable stories.
Manual, ISBN 08307.18834 $16.99

CASE STUDIES, TALK SHEETS AND DISCUSSION STARTERS

Teens learn best when they talk—not when you talk at them. A discussion allowing youth to discover the truth for themselves, with your guidance, is a powerful experience that will stay with them for a lifetime.
Manual, ISBN 08307.18842 $16.99

GAMES, CROWDBREAKERS AND COMMUNITY BUILDERS

Dozens of innovative, youth-group-tested ideas for fun and original crowdbreakers, as well as successful plans and trips for building a sense of community in your group.
Manual, ISBN 08307.18818 $16.99

More Resources for Youth Workers, Parents & Students

NATIONAL INSTITUTE OF YOUTH MINISTRY — NIYM

Steering Them Straight
Stephen Arterburn & Jim Burns

Parents can find understanding as well as practical tools to deal with crisis situations. Includes guidelines that will help any family prevent problems before they develop.
UPC 156179.4066 $10.99

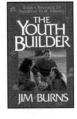

The Youth Builder
Jim Burns

This Gold Medallion Award winner provides you with proven methods, specific recommendations and hands-on examples of handling and understanding the problems and challenges of youth ministry.
ISBN 089081.1576. $16.95

Spirit Wings
Jim Burns

In the language of today's teens, these 84 short devotionals will encourage youth to build a stronger and more intimate relationship with God.
ISBN 08928.37837 $10.95

Radical Love
Book & Video, Jim Burns

In *Radical Love* kids discover why it's best to wait on God's timing, how to say no when their bodies say yes and how to find forgiveness for past mistakes.
Paperback, ISBN 08307.17935 $9.99
VHS Video, SPCN 85116.00922 $19.99

90 Days Through the New Testament
Jim Burns

A growth experience through the New Testament that lays the foundation for developing a daily time with God.
ISBN 08307.14561 $9.99

Getting in Touch with God
Jim Burns

Develop a consistent and disciplined time with God in the midst of hectic schedules as Jim Burns shares with you inspiring devotional readings to deepen your love of God.
ISBN 08908.15208 $2.95

Radical Christianity
Book & Video, Jim Burns

Radical Christianity is a proven plan to help youth live a life that's worth living and make a difference in their world.
Paperback, ISBN 08307.17927 $9.99
VHS Video, SPCN 85116.01082 $19.99

The Youth Worker's Book of Case Studies
Jim Burns

Fifty-two true stories with discussion questions to add interest to Bible studies.
ISBN 08307.15827 $12.99

To order NIYM resources, please call
1-800-397-9725
or to learn how you can take advantage of NIYM training opportunities call or write to:
NIYM • PO Box 297 • San Juan Capistrano
CA 92675 • 949/487-0217

What in the world is *NIYM*?

A.) The Neurotically Inclined Yo-Yo Masters
B.) The Neatest Incidental Yearbook Mystery
C.) The Natural Ignition Yields of Marshmallows
D.) The National Institute of Youth Ministry

If you deliberately picked A, B, or C you're the reason Jim Burns started NIYM! If you picked D, you can go to the next page. In any case, you could learn more about NIYM. Here are some IQ score-raisers:

Jim Burns started NIYM to:
• Meet the growing needs of training and equipping youth workers and parents
• Develop excellent resources and events for young people—in the U.S. and internationally
• Empower young people and their families to make wise decisions and experience a vital Christian lifestyle.

NIYM can make a difference in your life and enhance your youth work skills through these special events:

Institutes—These consist of week-long, in-depth small-group training sessions for youth workers.

Trainer of Trainees—NIYM will train you to train others. You can use this training with your volunteers, parents and denominational events. You can go through the certification process and become an official NIYM associate. (No, you don't get a badge or decoder ring).

International Training—Join NIYM associates to bring youth ministry to kids and adults around the world. (You'll learn meanings to universal words like "yo!" and "hey!")

Custom Training—These are special training events for denominational groups, churches, networks, colleges and seminaries.

Parent Forums—We'll come to your church or community with two incredible hours of learning, interaction and fellowship. It'll be fun finding out who makes your kids tick!

Youth Events—Dynamic speakers, interaction and drama bring a powerful message to kids through a fun and fast-paced day. Our youth events include: This Side Up, Radical Respect, Surviving Adolescence and Peer Leadership.

For brain food or a free information packet about the National Institute of Youth Ministry, write to:

NIYM
P.O. Box 297 • San Juan Capistrano, CA 92675
Tel: (949) 487-0217 • Fax: (949) 487-1758 • Info@niym.org